THE HEAVEN ON EARTH CONFERENCE:

THE WONDROUS DIARY OF AN ORDINARY PASTOR

KEES POSTMA

PROLOGUE

I have dedicated myself to keep a diary so that the rabble can get a glimpse into my extraordinary life. An invitation, almost too good to be true, is at the heart of this endeavour. It looks like I'm being pulled out of the swamp of mediocrity. I will tell you all about it later this week. For the next couple of months, I hope to blow you away with all the things God will do through me for the benefit of others.

My intuition tells me that this diary will prove to be beneficial for many. It will most certainly be a challenge for my readers not to be eaten up by jealousy. But I suppose the Lord will deal with these poor souls on a one-to-one basis. This shouldn't get into the way of me writing this masterpiece. Last night, I dreamed about those Bedouins who uncovered the Dead Sea scrolls almost a century ago. Some say it's the biggest archaeological discovery of the twentieth century. Perhaps, in a hundred years' time, this diary will be granted the same privilege. Who can tell? With my mind's eye, I can see ecstatic believers blowing the dust of this journal. Retrieving it from underneath a tree where it was safely buried and preserved somewhere in the Dutch Bible belt. They open and read, and their heart's desire is to return to the old paths of this diary writer. It was quite hard to fall asleep and even harder to remain modest after this dream, or was it a vision from the heavenlies? Sometimes it's hard to distinguish my own pride, deep down in the dungeons of my heart, from God's prompting and leading.

Deborah, my wife, stressed that this should be an honest diary, though. She's convinced that the next generations of faithful followers will learn more from my mistakes and insecurities than from a pastor who seems to have it all together. She mentioned something about pride coming before the fall, not sure why she thought this was the right time to pour cold water on my head. "Case, please don't take yourself too seriously, okay?"

A year has passed since my adventurous retreat in Ireland that I've documented in my first book: *The Retreat: A Light-Hearted and Humorous Story about a Soul-Searching Pastor*. And what a year it has been. I'm glad to inform you that Deborah and I have moved on.

I'm no longer pastoring the church of the Reformed Evangelical Seventh-Day Baptists of the Latter-Day Saints in the city of Utrecht. The sweet words of a Frisian pastoral search committee drew me in. Deborah needed more convincing. The parsonage, including a new kitchen and an infinity pool, did the trick for her, although she will never admit it. She also got an offer for a permanent position as a Primary School teacher and didn't have to think twice about it. So, this means we've pitched our tent in the county of Friesland, serving Zwagerheide First Baptist Church. Zwagerheide is only a dot on the map with ten thousand inhabitants tucked away in a lovely forest-like area in the north of Holland.

Our departure from Utrecht was heartbreaking, by the way. The news hit them like a bolt from the blue. When our farewell service was finished, we stepped into our minivan, and in the rearview mirror, I could see people waving and crying. Some of the men were starting a fire, probably so that they could throw ashes and burn their clothes as a sign of deep and profound mourning. At least, that's my reading.

Deborah and my oldest son have interpreted it differently. They agreed that people were crying, but they saw tears of joy. Mainly because they all formed a conga line during their "lament" and were setting off fireworks. Deborah and my son have always been "glass half empty" kind of people. Be that as it may, it will not be easy for the people in Utrecht to find a replacement for a spiritual giant like me. They're big shoes to fill. Welcome to the wondrous diary of an ordinary pastor.

FEBRUARY 2

It's time for me to hit the hay. Early to bed and to rise makes a man healthy, wealthy, and wise. Deborah is already asleep. I'm a bit reluctant to join her, to be honest. The day started off well. I managed to spend half an hour reading the Bible, praying, and memorizing a Bible verse. Every now and then, He chooses to show us a glimpse of His work within us. I felt very spiritual. I had written the verse down and put it in my pocket in case I forgot it, which is very unlikely. Again, I couldn't help but thinking about all those people who will read this diary, deciding for themselves to burn the candle at both ends to take the Word in just like me.

A few hours later, I found myself in a lingerie boutique on the outskirts of town. Judge not, that ye be not judged, Christian people. Let me explain the reason for this shopping spree. Deborah has been complaining for years that her friends always brag about their husbands buying something nice for them in this shop. Up until now, I've always come home empty handed. I've tried to reason with her that lurking around this store's "private seductive collection" is not appropriate for a shepherd of my stature. To make this very clear: I have no problem seeing all the nakedness on the artwork, but you never know what my sheep think when they see their spiritual father wandering around here like this. Mission accomplished, by the way. I couldn't wait for the look in her eyes when she unpacked her present!

At lunchtime, I already felt a little less spiritual. This had nothing to do with my shopping endeavour. Let me be clear about that. No, I read the newsletter of the Janmaat family. Deborah and I support them financially with a few nickels and dimes (we are saving up for a new campervan ourselves) in their attempt to reach some tribes in the Pacific with the Gospel. While I was reading their personal updates, I couldn't help but doubt my own usefulness for the Lord.

* * *

John Janmaat (39)

Beloved! Words can't describe what has happened to us this week. While we were playing hide and seek with our two rascals, we stumbled upon an unreached indigenous tribe. Betty used the bridge illustration to gently persuade the tribal chief to receive Christ, and so he did. We started a translation project for the Old and New Testament the day after. Ruben and Rebekka are leading this project. They are our pride and joy! It's fun to see them debating about translating the book of Malachi into this formerly unknown tribal language. Recently, I received a message from the Vatican. They intend to nominate me for canonization. I will be the first living non-Catholic Baptist missionary to receive such an honor because of our fruitful labor here over the years. I'm still considering, not sure what to do. Will you join me in prayer?

Betty Janmaat (32)

Dear daughters of the Most High. A special word for you ladies. Last week, some biblical archaeologists visited me. They followed me around for five days and came to the unanimous conclusion that I am probably the woman mentioned in Proverbs 31! Their final report brought tears to my eyes: "Her children rise and call her blessed; her husband also, and he praises her: Many women have done excellently, but you surpass them all."

Chances are that my picture and name will be included in the footnote of an updated version of the Woman's Study Bible. Before I forget, here's a little update on the two troublemakers of the family.

Rebekka Janmaat (4)

Rebekka is flourishing. John helped her with her Hebrew exam this week, and she passed with flying colours. The seminary over here has asked her if she would like to teach a bit of Hebrew in between her naps. She herself indicates that this is a matter of prayer for her, as she is afraid it may conflict with her ministry among the Swalineze toddlers. We uploaded a video for your enjoyment of Rebekka on our YouTube channel. You will see her reciting Romans. But as you know, with children, not all that glitters is gold. Last night I heard her sneaking out of her room at 2:00 a.m. When we confronted her the next morning with this act of disobedience, she apologized and explained that she went out to sit on the porch to pray for you all. It was hard for me and John to decide if we should discipline or praise her. We'd like to hear how you guys deal with this kind of parental trouble.

Ruben Janmaat (13)

They say that clergymen's sons always turn out badly. Our Ruben is turning into a rebellious teenager. The other day, we asked him to take the garbage out. Before we knew it, he had taken the neighbor's garbage out as well! The Lord had shown him that his good works should be known to everyone. Be that as it may, John and I are still trying to get our heads around the fact that Ruben seems to be unable to do exactly what we tell him to do. He has turned down an offer for his first professional contract as a footballer because he's convinced that the Mammon might get a grip on him. He's doing fine at school. He's the youngest student at his university, doing a major in Pauline theology. As a side hustle, he's paraphrasing the New Testament to rhyme in order that a group of rappers over here, suffering from dyslexia, may be able to understand the Word.

Before I forget. John had a vision last night. He saw someone. It could well be a pastor. He had a grim look on his face, and evil was all around him. He was driving a new campervan and doing a burnout while laughing hysterically. We felt burdened to share this vision in our newsletter. Maybe the Lord wants to speak to one of our supporters. Who knows? Well, that's us for now! Grace be unto you; may the Lord bless you as He blesses us.

I was about to send them an angry letter about how important it is to remain humble, especially when your core business is converting tribes. But I decided that speaking is silver, and silence is gold. I hope one of their supporters has the gift of discernment and will delay buying a new campervan.

* * *

Just after lunch, Deborah came home. I was very disappointed, to say the least. At first, I could see the joy and anticipation in her eyes when she saw the pink-and-white bag with a black bow on the table. Once she had unwrapped it, though, her face turned into what looked like an emerging thunderstorm. Apparently, her friends' husbands knew exactly what women want, but I was from a different planet. As she slammed the door loudly, I could just make out her saying that if I ever bought her shapewear again, she'd change the locks on the front door and every other door I could use to get near her. Well, pressure brings diamonds. That's also true for marriage, I suppose. To make matters worse, I probably had left a window open today. My entire wardrobe, including all the coat hangers, was all over the front lawn. Must have been a local windshear.

Now that I've entrusted my first day to you, dear diary, it's safe to say that the couch will probably be the best option for me tonight.

FEBRUARY 3

Okay, let's get down to business. I'm going to satisfy your curiosity. It's a privilege for me to announce that I've been invited as the keynote speaker for this year's Heaven on Earth Conference. The annual highlight for the most exuberant, enthusiastic Christians in my part of the world. Every year thousands upon thousands travel to this conference to enjoy seminars, limited sleep, and dodgy sanitary facilities while camping in leaky tents. Strangely enough, it's also often the place where God seems to do a special work in people.

They're expecting just over ten thousand people to turn up for this festival. What a day it that will be. That I, Case Parker, will walk onto the biggest stage possible for Dutch preachers! For most of my life, even after coming to Christ, I have felt inferior. I was the son that stayed in his bitterness, and the son that went away. I was the seed that fell among the thorns, the house built on the sand. I was the friend who tore everything to pieces with one kiss, the leper who didn't return. The rich young ruler who left disappointed. I was the blind man who wanted to see, the deaf man who wanted to hear. It wasn't until last year that I realized that the fattened calf was being prepared for me too. That the ring was also put on my finger and that the cloak also covered my sin and shame. That inferior mindset is now just water under the bridge.

Up until now, I'd only received invites from small and obscure churches to come and preach. Often during summer break, when the more gifted and eloquent public orators enjoyed their holidays. I found an old letter in my email from one such church inviting me to come and speak. It surely tells you how the people thought of me before. I can't wait to see the surprise on their faces when they see me shining on stage in a couple of months' time.

* * *

Dear C-list itinerant preacher,

All our A- and B- list preachers were busy doing other far more important things. How wonderful it is, then, that you have the humility to serve us, even though you know you are our last resort. We strongly believe that the Spirit blows where we want Him to go. In other words, we'd like to give Him all the room necessary within our own framework. That's why we think it's right to share our set of rules and regulations so that you won't stand in His way.

Date: May 4 (two days from now)
Theme: Worm (see sermon series)
Fee: To be agreed upon (see fee)

A. Appropriate clothing and hairstyle
You are required to conform to our clothing and hairstyle regulations regarding itinerant preachers. The founding mother of our congregation, sister C(aroline) Razy, in a vision, saw someone climbing our pulpit in a white shirt with blue shorts underneath and matching stockings worn just above the knee. We

take her insights very seriously and strongly suggest you follow them. In the unlikely event that these pieces are not in your wardrobe, you can rent a set, in the size you prefer, for €50,00 per Sunday.

Next to this, your hairstyle is of the utmost importance to us. Our sister was very clear on this as well. You can choose between two tonsures. The first is what we call the St. Peter tonsure: Shaving the top of the head, making sure there is plenty of hair on the sides. Your second option is the St. Paul tonsure: Shaving the sides, making sure there is plenty left on top. We have a shave and cut tutorial on our website. If you do not comply with either of them, our local hairdresser will do the job for you. This will cost you an additional €25,00.

B. Entering the church hall

As we sing our first song of worship, you and the elders enter the sanctuary. Please make sure to follow the well-ordered, regular, and synchronized formation that the elders have demonstrated for nearly half a century. Please come to a standstill near the pulpit, facing east, reaching out your hand. The elder who will hand you the announcements, Br. Janssen, will shake your hand and wish you all the best. Please touch his hand, but don't squeeze it. He has severe arthritis and carpal tunnel syndrome in the tip of his index finger on his right hand. Alternatively, you can shake his other hand, but please be aware of his golfer's elbow. Consultation beforehand is possible during your haircut.

C. The announcements

There are a number of announcements you must make; you can find them in our printed church bulletin. Please pray specifically and passionately for three of our members.

Brother Adrianus Thomassen à Thuessink van der Hoop van Slochteren (the third)

Brother Ovuvuevuevuve Enyetuenwuevuee Ugbemugbem Osassin (jr.)

Sister Carla Janssen

Two of them have indicated to the board of elders that they find it disturbing when their names aren't properly pronounced. Fortunately, we haven't received a complaint so far from our beloved sister Janssen.

D. Liturgy

In being the C-list iterant preacher, it is your responsibility to pick the songs. Again, we trust in the Spirit's guidance, nevertheless we think it's wise to set some boundaries here so that you don't offend Him in any way.

First, we prohibit singing songs with geographical references. So, any song with mountains, valleys, deserts, streams, trees, grass, or any other product of nature is off the menu.

Secondly, we only sing songs within a 3/4 rhythm signature. We understand this needs some explanation from our end. Here's what happened. Our organist went to a rather charismatic conference the other day. He had severe back pain and as he moved forward for prayer, one of the preachers told him that his legs were of uneven length. Regrettably, they accidentally prayed for the longer leg to grow. There is now a size difference of over thirty centimeters. He has indicated that, given this physical setback, a 3/4 rhythm best corresponds with his ability to press the organ pedals at the right time.

E. Sermon series

We expect you to preach on the theme assigned to you. As we've welcomed spring to our beautiful part of the world, we decided to do a sermon series on animals we find in Scripture.

April 28: Donkey Br. Don Key (British self-proclaimed evangelist)

May 4: Worm Br. C. Parker (Utrecht)

May 11:Fish Br. Fischer (Anabaptist preacher from Munich)

May 18:Eagle Br. Byrd (Dublin)

Considering your current track record in ministry, we thought that worm would be appropriate for you to preach on.

F. Fee

Freely you have received; freely you should give. But if you're still unaware that money is the root of all evil, you are more than welcome to send an invoice. In order not to embarrass you, we want you to know in advance that all our itinerant preachers, including those on our A-list, have waived their remuneration so that everything goes to one of our three charities:

1. Stray cats in Andalusia, Spain. We travel to Spain every year to catch stray cats and bring them to a local asylum. The annual costs for deworming, vaccination, food, and finding them a new place to live amount to around €3,500.

2. Guide dogs for the blind in Liechtenstein. We are proud to have been involved here for forty years. Unfortunately, the first dog we trained has already died without being deployed. According to the charities' management, which is somewhat difficult to reach, there are no blind people in Liechtenstein now. Nevertheless, we continue this good work so that a guide dog is immediately available should anyone become blind: Estimated cost is about €14,600 on an annual basis.

3. Retirement home for pastors. We see it as an incredible opportunity that five years ago, just a stone's throw from Chernobyl, Ukraine, we were able to buy an apartment building for the

symbolic sum of €1. Many retired itinerant speakers of our B and C list are now housed here. At the moment, we are working on the "Running Water" project, to provide running water in all flats. Last year, partly due to preachers' donations, a glow-in-the-dark vegetable garden was opened near the former nuclear factory site.

There's an exception to every rule they say, but not with us.

We are looking forward to seeing you in a couple of days. If you waive your fee, we ask you to bring €75 in cash for the outfit and the haircut. We wish you all the best as you meticulously prepare your message within the boundaries mentioned in this letter.

Love, grace, and peace,
The board of elders

* * *

Now you'll understand why I'm glad those days belong to the past. I trust history won't repeat itself. I can't wait to start preparing my sermon for the Heaven on Earth conference!

February 4

I've been eating some humble pie and received the silent treatment for the last two days, but Deborah and I are finally on speaking terms again. She has the gift of bearing with all my stupidities. She also notices my upcoming storms of self-glorification before I can feel the first breeze myself.

"Honey, please promise me you won't get too carried away, okay?" Without awaiting my reply, she picks up her Bible. "I was reading a passage this morning, and it reminded me about your upcoming conference debut. It says: 'If anyone imagines that he knows something, he does not yet know as he ought to know. But if anyone loves God, he is known by God.' I know your imagination probably runs wild now. You picture yourself on one of those conference posters around churches throughout Holland. You see yourself giving interviews to the papers and magazines. But please take this advice from your humble, and pretty, wife: All the knowledge you think you have falls short of being known by Him, okay? Well, I hope you let that sink in. Could you please take out the garbage and empty the dishwasher for me?"

I smile at her and start my chores. Without Deborah, I would've ended up with an ego on steroids, that's for sure. By the way, I'm going out with Marcel tomorrow to keep my end of a promise I made to him last year.

FEBRUARY 5

I woke up early today, a tiny bit nervous I have to say. Marcel, my best friend and one of Holland's celebrity preachers, picked me up. You might remember that I made him a promise on Tramore Beach. As the Lord dealt with me there like He never did before, Marcel had seen me crying out to Him. When I told him what had happened, he asked me if I was willing to share this experience at the Victorious Fruitful Female conference where he was asked to preach. I hesitated but decided to give it a go.

Today's the day to travel to the town of Vrouwenparochie to get vulnerable and open myself up for, I assume, thousands of women ready to take in some of my wisdom and insight. A journey of a thousand miles begins with a single step. This is my first!

"Good to see you, Case. Are you ready to go? Have you written your outline in the palm of your hand?"

"Yes, my friend, ready when you are!" Even though I'm still somewhat hiding behind my carefully created mask of humor and indifference, God started a great and new work in me the year before. It's like the sun rising and freeing itself from the clouds that cover her. Or like a red rose budding above the thorns.

Cornelius O'Hallihan and Eileen Kennedy, our retreat leaders, were used as tools in the Carpenter's tool belt, sharing their stories. Since then, I know I'm loved, known, and wanted. Loved because someone died for me while I was still a sinner. Known, for he knows and searches my inner being. Wanted, for he wants me to be where He is.

Earlier on in my Christian life, I only felt loved when I got good reviews on my online sermons, known when I had the attention of people, and wanted when bigger churches informed me they wanted me to come and teach. I must confess I still sometimes search horizontally for what has been given to me vertically: love, acceptance, amazing grace. But I did sense a clear turning point after my retreat.

Even Deborah says I'm much more relaxed than I was before. That I've started living as a beloved child of the Father instead of a hardworking employee of "the grumpy boss upstairs." She promised she will be my gatekeeper. When I backslide to the point where God becomes small and people become big again, she won't hesitate to act. I do hope that the preaching today and the preparation for the conference won't throw a wrench in the works.

I'm not the only one who came back a changed man after the retreat. Using Marcel's own words: I'm not who I was before, but I'm becoming who I already am in Christ. Three days away from the spotlights and under God's Word worked miracles in his life too. His growing ministry had put wool over his eyes throughout the years. He knew how to wind people around his fingers in an instant but got convicted that he had taken them down with him in some sort of shallow easy believism. After returning, he canceled most of his speaking engagements and postponed his book launch. Instead of the spotlights of Christian ministry, he chooses candlelight lit dinners with his wife, Miriam.

He realized that the sculptor Michelangelo was right. The story goes that he was once approached by a woman while he was sculpting a beautiful horse. "Sir, isn't it very difficult to sculpt a horse from such a rock?" Michelangelo smiled and said, "Madam, it's quite easy. After all, the horse is already in there. I just have to chip away the rest and then the horse remains."

As far as Marcel and I are concerned, this is a brilliant illustration of what God has been doing in our lives since the retreat. He's shaping and molding us. Carving everything away, until only Christ is left. The retreat has given us both a new lease of life.

"Can you explain to me why these conferences always have these ridiculous, long names?" I asked him somewhere halfway round the new beltway around our province capital, Leeuwarden.

"Sure, my friend. First, most of them are in English because it sounds more important and interesting. If you're having a hard time pronouncing the theme, it must be interesting, right? Secondly, you want to communicate a certain amount of positivity, preferably with alliteration. Try to put yourself in Deborah's shoes: I'm sure she wants to be victorious and fruitful!"

"Well, she's very down to earth, Marcel. I think she'd rather have her wisdom teeth pulled than go to conferences like these, but I could be wrong." As we drove past the military airport on the outskirts of the little town of Stiens, I decided to tell Marcel my breaking news. "You probably won't believe this, but I've been asked to speak at the Heaven on Earth conference this year. Not in a seminar tucked away in the back of the conference center where the mouse droppings are and it smells like the sewer, but on the main stage! Can you believe it? Me,

Case Parker, speaker at our country's biggest Christian event. How about that, brother?"

Marcel seemed lost for words. He sat quietly for a moment, tapping his fingers on the steering wheel of his Volvo V70. "Case, do you remember our time at Calumn's, on our last day in Ireland where we learned the lesson of the Dicentra Spectabilis, also known as the 'flower of the broken heart?' Do you remember how that flower thrives best in the shadows instead of in the burning daylight? That's not only true for flowers but also for us pastors. You haven't forgotten that right? Please hear me out, Case. I don't want to pour cold water on your news; I'm thrilled for you to have this opportunity. I will be praying for you and offer you my help and advice and will be there every step of the way. But working toward a momentum like this has a downside as well. It's like dancing on a minefield, skating on thin ice. It nearly killed my faith, as you know. The gold, glory, fortune, and fame can have a negative impact; that's all I'm trying to say."

I could hear in his tone of voice that he was concerned for my wellbeing, like a friend sharpening iron with iron.

Before I could answer, he asked, "What's Deborah take on this?"

"Well, she's happy I've been given the chance. She also thinks I have something to say to the masses, but I had to promise her I won't get carried away by all of this."

"She's a wise woman. I see eye to eye with her on this one."

At that point, we had reached our destination: Vrouwenparochie (Women's Parish in English). A small dot on the map in the Frisian district of the Bildt. Famous for its potatoes, it's a place where the salty smell of the sea is always present. We parked at the indoor sports center.

"Tell me, Marcel, is there a special backdoor entrance for preachers like me? Did you manage to get me that bowl of blue M&M's for my dressing room?"

Marcel smiled. The parking lot was desolated, I couldn't see any flags, posters, banners, or traffic controllers. At first sight, it didn't look victorious and fruitful at all.

As we entered the hallway, I could see a sign saying Tennis Courts. I chose to go over and check the stage where I would be sharing my wisdom later on. When I opened the door, some middle-aged men were practicing their serve. "Are you sure that we're in the right place, Marcel?"

"Case, not all conferences draw big crowds, you know."

The janitor walked up as he saw us wandering around and decided to show us the way. We climbed the stairs and took the first door on the right, which led, to my disappointment, to a rather small room. About thirty women had gathered and were enjoying their coffee in a poorly heated room. "Well, if these are the victorious fruitful females, there's little hope for the church, don't you think?"

"One who is faithful in a very little is also faithful in much, and one who is dishonest in a very little is also dishonest in much, Case. Don't despise the small things. Maybe you should take these women as seriously as the thousands upon thousands next May." Marcel replied, tone serious.

It was time to start, it seemed. I tried breaking the ice. "Hello ladies, it's a privilege for me to be in your midst. My name is Case Parker, forty-eight years of age, quite young from your perspective, and I have one wife and two children. If it had been the other way around, we should have a very different conversation, don't you think?"

Zero response. They all looked at me like I had just been reading all the possible side-effects for a painkiller. "Well, I've been asked to share with you about the power of vulnerability. I've decided to read some portions of my first book to explain to you what happened to me last year at Tramore Beach. Can you please put up my first slide?"

My charming assistant and personal driver put up my first

and only slide, then decided to dim the lights a little. That was a mistake. This seemed to trigger a severe outbreak of narcolepsy. With every sentence read, I noticed someone going down into the twilight zone.

It brought me back to my sleepovers with my uncle Vincent. He had a rather large birdcage filled with canaries. When he would cover the cage with a towel, removing the light from their presence, they would all go to sleep. After reading a page or two, I decided to close the book.

The victorious, fruitful women of Vrouwenparochie continued to snore in close harmony. Marcel and I decided to sneak out. When we were back in the car, Marcel could no longer control himself. I gave him a piece of my mind by telling him that laughing out loud at someone else's misfortunate wasn't a very Christian thing to do. Though, admittedly, I'd probably do the same if it had been the other way around. Well, there's always tomorrow.

FEBRUARY 7

This might sound a bit creepy, but one of the first things I do after moving is visit the local graveyard. The one in Zwagerheide is situated on the outskirts of town. It surrounds a beautiful medieval church that has been going back and forth in ownership between Catholics and Protestants for ages. As I looked around, I could see thousands of graves. Some of them recent—a small hill with some flowers and probably fresh tears on them. Others are over two hundred years old, where no one has shed a tear in decades. All these people proved to be replaceable. All things must come to an end.

Looking at it that way, speaking at a conference isn't that big of a deal after all. Some of the graves, mainly the older ones, have Bible verses inscribed. Others have opted for Clapton or

Sting's inspiration, telling me about tears in heaven and fields of gold.

While the sun and clouds were casting their shadows on the graveyard, I couldn't help but think about the engraving on my tombstone when I must go the way of this earth. I read a verse today that made me very uneasy. It's about King Amaziah who reigned over Israel for nearly thirty years. Here's the short summary of his life:

Amaziah was twenty-five years old when he began to reign, and he reigned twenty-nine years in Jerusalem. His mother's name was Jehoaddan of Jerusalem. And he did what was right in the eyes of the Lord, yet not with a whole heart. (2 Chr. 25:2, ESV)

I can imagine someone walking through that graveyard, in forty years' time, stopping at my temporary place of rest, and reading this on my tombstone: "In loving memory of Case Parker. He did what was right in the eyes of the Lord, yet not with a whole heart." On second thought, maybe I should just go with Clapton or Sting. Must tell Deborah. You never know when it's your last day, do you?

FEBRUARY 8

I had planned to keep this diary cheerful, light-hearted, and entertaining, but I'm afraid that won't happen. I got a call this morning from the Boersma family. Precious living stones of the spiritual house that I am building here, under His leadership. They asked me if I could come down for a quick cup of coffee to discuss something important. I gave Deborah a hug, took my bike out of the garage, and cycled over the cobbled lanes. There was some snow last night, and I could see the local children taking advantage. They withstood the urge to throw a snowball at their pastor, and as a result, I reached the Boersmas' in one piece.

"Glad you're here, brother Parker, please sit down."

Marjolein directed me to a sunny spot in their newly built conservatory. Johan did the job himself. He's a quiet man whose most recognizable future is his two hands. I had noticed that when he skillfully designed and built custom bookcases in our parsonage.

"We all have our own unique talents and gifting, Pastor. I happen to be good in carpentry," he told me as he helped us move in.

I told him that it's one of the first spiritual gifts mentioned in the Bible in the story of Bezalel and Oholiab, two spirit-filled craftsmen, who were called to build the Tabernacle. From that moment on, we got on great. I made sure to tell him, though, that the body of Christ indeed is helped with two hands but can't function without masterminds like me.

While I'm nestled in next to a pellet stove that easily defeats the cold from outside, Johan and Marjolein sat in the other two chairs. They looked nervous.

A toddler danced around in the living room like only toddlers can—singing their own songs, living in their own world. She sang like she was the only one in the universe.

As I reflected on Jesus's words about becoming like one of these little ones, I readied myself for the impending revelations from Johan and Marjolein. I've often sat in a chair like that one. In some strange way, people have always felt safe to confide in me.

I've heard many secrets that have been locked in the dungeons of many hearts for way too long. Stories about adultery, physical abuse, and suicidal thoughts come to mind. I've often felt like a square peg put in a round hole, unable to solve these problems in people's lives. Like a firefighter coming to the scene with only a garden hose at his disposal. I've encouraged my congregations to come to me when they notice the smoke starting to rise instead waiting until flames are coming through every window, but many have failed to adhere to that wise counsel.

When I started off years ago, I thought my job was to explain the Bible and love people. Looking back at nearly twenty years of ministry, I feel the role has changed. People expect me to be a theologian, a visionary, a team builder, a social worker, a psychologist, and a budget coach. They want to be great in the goal but also score goals at the other end of the field. Maybe it's not what they expect but a yoke that I've put on myself as the years have gone by. His yoke is easy, and His burden is light. Mine is heavy and difficult to carry at times.

"Brother Parker, let's get straight to it. There's something troubling us, but we were a bit reluctant sharing it with you before. Johan and I wanted you to have a smooth transition from Drenthe to Zwagerheide."

I thanked them for their understanding but assured them that we've settled in just fine and were ready to dig in a bit deeper at this stage.

"Our little Salomé is not doing well, brother."

I turned my head. The little girl in the living room had just started a roleplay with her dolls. What could possibly be wrong if you were floating through life like she was?

"In the last six months, she kept getting headaches and spells of dizziness, which increased as time passed. When she played with the kids in the street, she was the first to come in complaining about how tired she was. We went to see the doctor. She's our first and only child, so we don't have any other kids for comparison. The doctor told us that he couldn't find anything wrong with her, but when she also got bruises for no apparent reason, our GP referred us to the hospital in Leeuwarden. To keep a long story short, two weeks ago they diagnosed her with acute lymphocytic leukemia." For a moment, Marjolein was unable to continue, tears running down her face.

Johan placed his hand on her knee and gazed outside of the window at the still-falling snow. "It felt like the ground was slipping under our feet, pastor."

It wasn't the first time in my ministry that I felt like being the wrong person for the job. Verses saying that, in all things, God will work things for the good become hollow phrases to many receiving devastating news like this. They're as powerful as trying to stop a bullet with a handkerchief.

Our eyes met for a short while; I was lost for words. I stood from my chair and decided to hug them both. The three of us cried for a minute or two, and I ended with a short prayer asking the Giver of Life to comfort us all. I sensed that both appreciated my helplessness. Gazing through my tears, I saw Salomé curiously staring at the three grown-ups crying. As if she couldn't understand why one would cry when the snow was coming down and a possibility had arisen to build a snowman with Daddy. Playing in the storm, dancing in the rain.

February 9

I woke up early today, rough night. Deborah eventually came to find me; she probably noticed my part of the bed was empty. "Are you worrying again, ye of little faith?" She sat next to me.

"Yes, I woke up at 3:15, like I often do. It's probably the full moon; you know how that affects my sleeping pattern."

She looked at me and smiled. "We both know that's not the reason, Case. You're desperately trying to get your head around what happened yesterday. Being the man that you are, you're probably trying to find a way to fix the situation. The last time the Lord was looking for a Messiah, He didn't call you, did He? Why can't you just accept that, on this side of eternity, things are not perfect, and you're only called and equipped to come alongside? You told me yesterday evening that Salomé kept on singing, 'Let it go, let it go.' Maybe you should do the same for once in your life."

I reckoned it was a bit early to get a discussion going about the fact of whether God could speak through Disney movies, but I heard what she was saying. "I'll give it a try honey, I promise."

FEBRUARY 13

These last couple of days have been extremely busy. I couldn't find time to write in my diary. Salomé has been in my thoughts twenty-four/seven, overshadowing the excitement of the conference. The elders and I got together last night to see how we could best serve the Boersmas in this difficult time. Their small group was already a step ahead of us. They decided to cook them a daily dinner so that Marjolein can focus on the hospital appointments and Johan can continue to work and provide for the family.

While gardening yesterday, my neighbor came over for a quick chat. "Parker, I don't doubt my unbelief and I have no immediate plans of doing so. But I can only praise your little flock for the way they care for the Boersmas."

My normal response would be to persuade him to visit church, but I decided to just thank him for the compliment. It was as if I heard the Spirit whispering:

A new commandment I give to you, that you love one another: just as I have loved you, you also are to love one another. By this all people will know that you are my disciples, if you have love for one another. (John 13: 34-35)

Tonight we've got our annual evangelism brainstorm scheduled. We are ready to reach Zwagerheide with some new out-of-the-box evangelistic tools. One of my elders told me that I shouldn't expect miracles. "Parker, we bark but usually don't bite. Don't get your hopes up too high, okay?"

You know, I really don't like the fact people pour cold water on my expectations without permission.

FEBRUARY 14

I was too exhausted yesterday to entrust anything to my journal. I decided to spend the evening with Deborah, binge watching an old British detective. In talking to other church leaders, I've found that drinking a proportionate amount of alcohol can be a great coping mechanism.

During fiery discussions with my sheep, my thoughts often go to a bag of M&M's, a British detective, and a Guinness. What I know now is that it's important to at least give the impression that I'm still listening. I do that by giving numerous examples of nonverbal consent. Like tilting my head thirty degrees or giving them a thumbs up. Nodding yes or pulling someone closer is also one of my tactics. Up until now, I've refrained from touching someone actively, which was suggested to me by my uncle Vincent. Anyway, this is my way of convincing people I'm still on board with where they want to go, without letting them know where I want to go.

Let's go back to our little get-together last night. One of the elders had warned me for a second time not to have high hopes. He even gave me a detailed outline of what was going to happen.

"Brother Parker, this is how it's going to go down tonight. Please listen carefully. It'll happen like clockwork. Before the break, we will be singing songs like 'Onward Christian Soldiers' and 'Shine, Jesus, Shine' from the top of our lungs. Then we'll grab the old whiteboard out and write our most creative ideas on evangelism on yellow sticky notes. At that stage, we are still extremely happy with ourselves and sense that it might be the Lord Himself leading us in new and unexpected ways. When the buzzer sounds, we all retreat into the hall where we'll drink lukewarm coffee and eat out-of-date Stroopwafels. Meanwhile, we start chatting about our kids who have fallen from the faith, our own burnouts, and the surplus of English songs sung by a traditional Baptist church like ours. Within a quarter of an hour, we have traveled back from the seventh heaven to plant our feet firmly in the muck and mire of life.

"When the buzzer sounds again, one of the elders encourages us to take our seats and asks us the million-dollar question for the night: Who would like to implement one of the ideas stuck on the whiteboard? It's hard to tell if the gift of hand raising is taken from the church at that specific moment, but no one has ever stepped forward to bring one of our magnificent ideas to life. Up until now, our evangelistic efforts are no bigger than opening the doors on Sunday morning." Elder Zwarts smiled at me, patted me on the shoulder, and wished me all the best.

"Thanks Brother Zwarts, I suppose forewarned is forearmed." Together we entered the sanctuary where a group of extremely excited Baptists were ready for their annual evangelism pitch.

I must admit that, based on the first half of the evening, I would have attributed the gift of prophecy to Zwarts. Something highly unlikely among Baptists. Everything happened just like he said it would. But to everyone's astonishment, something spectacular occurred. It was no other than Brother van Beelen who raised both hands, stood, and walked toward the front of the sanctuary. Everyone was silent as he took the microphone.

"Brothers and sisters, my proposal is that next month we will take matters into our own hands. We will take control of the pulpit! We will relieve our brother Parker from his duties that Sunday and immerse ourselves in some Bible-based building up of the saints. O ye of little faith and dull of heart, haven't you read 1 Corinthians 14:28? It says that when we come together, each one has a hymn, a lesson, a revelation, a tongue, or an interpretation. Well then, Baptists of Zwagerheide, we will have our first 'We all get to play church service,' and we'll invite as many unbelievers as we can."

The high-pitched noise, caused by van Beelen's frenzy, coming from the microphone was deafening. He scanned the crowd with his eyes wide open to observe if his idea was effective.

Some of my sheep were entranced and totally stunned that a useful idea came from this meeting. They stood, ran toward van Beelen, and jumped on him as if he had just scored the winning penalty in a World Cup final.

When everyone was back in their seats a few minutes later, the elders and I decided to give our go-ahead for the idea. March 20 will go down in history as the first interactive service of the Baptists of Zwagerheide. Although last night was a little bit weird, to say the least, I'm kind of looking forward to it. It's wonderful to serve and pastor an evangelistic crowd like this!

FEBRUARY 17

Marcel came by today to help me get started with my conference sermon. It's like beginning with kickboxing and having Rico Verhoeven to teach you the ropes! I've always looked up to Marcel. He once was Holland's most famous celebrity preacher, beating everyone to it. He served a church bigger than all the churches I've ever pastored combined. He's outgoing; I'm self-conscious. I come from the countryside of northeastern Holland, raised within a family of bog workers. He was born and raised with a silver spoon in his mouth in the suburbs of Amsterdam. You could say he was Paul, and I felt like the slightly weird cousin of Timothy. But things have changed.

Underneath Marcel's fame and fortune were more

insecurities than I'd ever imagined. He struggled with the expectations people had for him as his ministry grew. His theology proved to be a mile wide but only an inch deep. Walking with God, for him, felt like walking on thin ice. Looking at it that way, we weren't that different after all. But things have changed. God intervened, softened our hearts during a walk on one of Ireland's most beautiful beaches.

But old habits die hard, so I assumed he could still give me some dos and don'ts in regards to speaking before massive crowds. I needed to have some tricks up my sleeve to stand the test. There was only one chance to make a great first impression, and Marcel was just the man for the job to make that happen.

"Marcel, I've been doing some intelligent thinking about which passage would be fitting for my sermon. The showdown between Elijah and the Baal priests would be appealing to the crowds, I'd say. Or maybe the head-to-head between Moses and Pharaoh, or the day the sun stood still when Joshua fought a foreign army; what do you reckon? I need one of those miraculous, extraordinary, and epic heaven-on-earth narratives from Scripture to blow away the audience. Wait, David and Goliath may be a better fit. I can teach on three steps to kill your giants or something like that. I'm sure I'll have new followers eating out of my hand after that one!" I looked at Marcel for approval, like a puppy wagging its tail.

"Case, you're right. These stories are part and parcel of most sermons during these get-togethers. I can understand your thinking, especially because this is your debut of sorts." He put his hands behind his head, exhaled, and stared at me for a moment. "But this provides you with a momentous opportunity to break the deadlock. Instead of giving people what they want to hear, you can give them what they need to hear."

"And what do you think these people need to hear, my

friend?" I asked. To be honest, I wasn't sure; I was beginning to feel nervous over this whole endeavor.

"Case, I think that heaven touches earth, not only in our victorious moments, but especially at times when we suffer and go through hardship. Elijah, getting depressed after one of the greatest moments in his ministry. Job, losing his children. Jonah thrown off a boat into the deep sea. Jeremiah preaching for over forty years without anyone paying attention. Our Lord Himself crying out, 'Why have you forsaken me' during the anguish of the cross. What if you, Case Parker, make a case for how God deals with us in our times of pain, grief, and suffering? How He's near the brokenhearted and the contrite of spirit?" We sat in silence for a moment. He looked straight into my eyes, clearly not planning to avert his gaze before I responded.

"I'm not sure, Marcel. I'm afraid this will end my career as a conference speaker before it has started properly. Do you know how many people watch online and on-demand? This can haunt me forever, you know. Those Christian newspapers will eat me for breakfast!"

"Yes, my friend, I know, and I get what you're saying. But you can't make an omelet without breaking eggs. I'm not telling you what to do; I'm just asking you to consider it, okay? You haven't forgotten about Eileen's nugget of truth that she shared with us last year, have you? The purest gold is found in the muck and mire."

"Can't I do a bit of both, then? Some heroic stories and some painful ones?" I stutter.

"If you are chasing two hares, you won't catch either of them, my friend, so make up your mind."

The smell of Deborah and Miriam's cooking drew us away from our conversation and downstairs. They'd already prepared the table, so we sat down, dove in, and made small talk. A friend is sometimes closer than a brother, and iron sharpens iron. Isn't that what Scripture teaches?

FEBRUARY 19

The busiest day of the week is behind me. We a had a great turnout this Sunday morning. Most likely because of the trials of the Boersma family. Everyone wanted to hear the latest news on Salome's condition. Desperate times require desperate measures. During the Second World War here in Holland, the pews were filled with many anxious people, driven there due to despair. But in times of peace and security, numbers decreased quickly.

My uncle Vincent used to scornfully comment that, "When trials come, faith increases." I can still see him smoking his cigar while sharing that wisdom. This wasn't his way of encouraging people to go to church, but his disdain toward people who suddenly start believing in God when life throws them a curveball. "Faith in God is a crutch for weaklings, Case, remember that, son." I should pay him a visit soon; I am thinking of inviting him to our special "we all get to play" church service. Could be the Lord's prompting!

Life turned out differently than he had hoped. It wasn't unexpected for the rest of us: When you plant thorns, you shouldn't expect to gather roses. He became a jack of all trades and master of none and left a trail of broken marriages behind him. It turned him into a bitter man with a broken heart. I reckon he is the perfect lump of clay for the Potter's skilled hands.

I tried to aim for the heart instead of the head this morning to comfort Johan and Marjolein and the rest of the flock. I taught about some verses that had touched my own heart earlier this week.

During those many days the king of Egypt died, and the people of Israel groaned because of their slavery and cried out for help. Their cry for rescue from slavery came up to God. And God heard their groaning, and God remembered his covenant with

Abraham, with Isaac, and with Jacob. God saw the people of Israel—and God knew. (Ex. 2 23-25 ESV)

God heard, God remembered, and God knew. God, who intervenes on behalf of his people in the pain and anguish of everyday life. I got the impression that Johan and Marjolein were particularly touched by the fact that God knows. As a preacher, I often scan the room to see how people respond to my message. I saw Marjolein slipping her hand into Johan's as I was preaching this message of hope.

Little Salomé was playing in the back of our sanctuary. She had great fun with an older man who sat next to her, probably her grandpa or a family member of some sorts. He was in his late fifties, early sixties maybe. Gray hair, blue eyes, and one of those barber-trimmed beards.

Johan looked over his shoulder as Salomé giggled and had one of her imaginary conversations with her dolls. "Grandpa" winked at me a couple of times and nodded his head as if he wanted to say, "Go on, son, infuse some strength, and shine rays of hopes in these dark and difficult circumstances. They are not as strong as they think they are."

FEBRUARY 21

Marjolein sent me an email today asking if the elders and I wanted to come down to pray with Salomé and anoint her with oil. I really have a love-hate relationship with this practice, even though I know it's biblical. For the last fifteen years, I've prayed over many of the sick. None of them received physical healing. In one of my darker moments, I said to Deborah that if someone is at death's door and wants to die, they need to give me a call and I'll pray over them. Job done.

But at the same time, I've really enjoyed praying with people and counseling them in their last days on earth. Holding their hand, singing their favorite hymn, and knowing that God can do more than we pray for or can even imagine. The tears that mix with the oil, God being tangibly present.

I have worried that, because of my doubt, people have died. If only they had a pastor who was full of faith, they would still be playing with their grandchildren and making precious memories. Those thoughts have haunted me for years. My own doubt inflamed by the archenemy, the father of all lies.

I remember counselling an older lady who was going the way of all the earth. She was convinced she was going to be ninety; God had told her that. For five long years, she received cancer treatment. She was diagnosed with lung cancer without ever smoking a cigarette her entire life. She remained confident that she was going to be healed and amid it she continued to be an incredibly joyful and loving follower of Christ, despite her suffering. Eventually she died at the age of eighty-two, just short of seeing her third great-grandchild being born.

When I was standing next to her moments after she passed away, I realized God probably received more honor and glory from the way she went through her illness than if he had healed her miraculously. Countless people visited her, and she gave them a piece of heaven on earth. They got a glimpse into how suffering becomes bearable if you're being carried by God. Through her, they heard the voice of the Good Shepherd who continued to provide, even in the valley of death. Sometimes more can be seen in the night than during the day, especially when there's a bright light piercing through the darkness toward the edge of dawn.

Deborah and I have concluded that suffering and death are part of life. One way or the other, he seems it fit for us to go through the experience. As some sort of portal to a new world. Through it, we encounter a small part of what Christ has suffered for us.

Hey Marjolein, thanks for your message! Of course, we are glad to come down and pray over Salomé. We will have it

announced in church on Sunday so the church can pray as well.
Greetings to Johan and a big hug for Salomé. Talk soon. Blessings,
Case.

FEBRUARY 26

I visited my uncle Vincent today. I pulled myself together and
went to see him. He lives in a flat somewhere in a small town
where three of our counties border. The flat used to be an
annex for an elderly home, enabling the elderly to live
independently. Now it's a home to all sorts of people. Asylum
seekers who received their green card, single dads struggling to
get by, pensioners, and people like Vincent. A man in his late
fifties, ex-military, who spent most of his life shoveling dirt,
excavating building sites with only a shovel in his calloused
hands. His back and knees had enough of it when he had just
turned forty, and since then he has received unemployment
benefits. He was also a womanizer with the tendency to
overestimate his drinking ability.

I've been praying for him ever since I came to faith myself.
Sadly, he's still not doubting his unbelief. There are no fruit of
the Spirit to be seen. To be blunt, he's considered the black
sheep of the family. You probably have one of those sheep in
yours too. If you don't know who that is, you could be in a little
bit of a problem. Chances are it is you, but I can't be sure, so
don't get mad.

Vincent's life deteriorated as the old drink got the better of
him. He loved the odd pub fight, and married women have
always been his guilty pleasure, except for his own. Yet, with my
mind's eye, I saw Uncle Vincent coming to faith through a
psalm, teaching, or a dance at our "We all get to play" church
service. So, it was time to invite him personally.

As I made my way up, I stop at number 24. I looked
through the curtains to see if anyone was home. There he was.

A cigar on his lower lip, unshaved, sitting on his fake leather couch. A few bottles of cheap wine were on the table. I hoped that was for yesterday's meal and not his breakfast. He's stroking his cats, Gizmo and Gremlin, who join him in watching the telly. They're viewing one of those infomercials, trying to persuade us to avail of a once-in-a-lifetime offer so we can get a six-pack. I guess old Vincent's interest lies most with the young ladies demonstrating it.

I decided to interrupt the peaceful scene by gently knocking on the door.

Vincent looked up and stretched his knees. "David, boy, what a pleasure to have you. Now tell me, why have you come to see this old fellow? You probably have better things to do, haven't you?" Vincent may have lost some physical strength along the way, but his mind and tongue are still sharp and fast.

After politely refusing his kind offer to drink a barley smoothie, as he calls his beer, I sat. There were four chairs around an old mahogany table, but I think three of them were as good as new and never used. His sharp tongue turned many people away through the years, including three of his wives and four of his children. They've grown up to be young adults, but Vincent is not on speaking terms with them. One drunken outburst at a Christmas party was the straw that broke the camel's back. What's left are the pictures in his cabinet. All of them smiling and sitting together on Vincent's lap.

The last time I visited him was a year ago. I looked through the same curtains as I did today, and I saw him sitting at the table. His dark, yellow-stained fingers were caressing that photograph. He touched the photos as I heard his crying. I left without knocking and wondered how someone with such a big mouth could have such a tender heart. I am increasingly convinced the Gospel would fulfill so many of his needs. Forgiveness, acceptance, restoration, a clean slate, reconciliation to name a few.

"Uncle Vincent, I'm coming with a request, an invite of a kind. You may have heard that Deborah and I have moved to Zwagerheide to pastor a Baptist Church over there. We would love to have you over for a special service we are organizing in a few weeks' time. I think you will really like this one. There's no sermon, just a bit of banter and entertainment and food and beverages afterward. I think it's perfect for people like you. What do you say?".

Vincent looked at me; his smile tells me that I'm in for a bit of heat. "People like me, you say? By that, you mean stubborn and lonely unbelievers who see faith as a crutch for weak people. That's what you mean, Case, isn't it?"

"Well, I wouldn't use those exact words, but in fairness, yes. I promise that Deborah will cook her signature dish, beer-braised beef short ribs, for you to enjoy before or after the service. If that doesn't clinch the deal, I'd better go home straightaway."

"Fine, son, I'll be there. A bit of church won't harm me, I think."

I felt relieved. We continued to chitchat for half an hour, and then I left Vincent, Gizmo, and Gremlin to themselves. Will our first "We all get to play" church service go down into history as the day Uncle Vincent finally comes Home?

MARCH 1

Deborah agrees with Marcel. I hate when that happens. Now I'm outnumbered. "I think he's right, love. I really think you should speak about the fruitfulness of suffering. We don't always soar above the storms on eagle wings. Sometimes we must endure the full impact of a thunderstorm, and I think he has good reasons for it. It's the beauty and brokenness, the rise and fall of the Christian life. And please don't worry if you are not invited back. I think we'll manage without the €150 you get for fifty hours of sermon preparation. I'll find you some chores to do around the house for €3 an hour to bring in the cash."

I extremely dislike the fact that she questions my authority as provider for this godly home.

"Come here, Case, let me hit it right between your eyes." She opens her iPad and shows me a clip of Irish singer Sinead O'Connor, performing on Saturday Night live in October 1992. She's singing a version of Bob Marley's "War." In closing, she puts a picture of the pope in front of the camera, tears it apart, and speaks words that cannot be misinterpreted by the millions that are watching: "Fight the real enemy." She grew up in the Republic of Ireland, was abused as a young child by the church, and decided to stand up and speak out. She took the chance to give a voice to her inner child and became a voice for many who suffered abuse like she did, in different shapes and forms within the church during those dark years. Doing something with not a single clue what the consequences would be.

"Honey, how does this prove your point? You don't expect me to finish my sermon by tearing up a picture of some famous word-of-faith healers, do you? That would be slightly out of the ordinary, especially for the Baptists around!"

"No, silly, I don't want you arrested. What I'm saying is that you have an excellent opportunity to stand up for what needs to be said: That God allows suffering for the benefit of his children and the growth of their character. Why can't you be the twenty-first century Christian version of Sinead O'Connor? Do you remember how good it was to share our own story at last year's pastor's conference? And hearing the other pastors and pastors' wives sharing theirs?" Deborah reached for her notebook, ready to slam it home. She started reading the notes she'd made as shepherd after shepherd poured their heart out:

"Slander caused a lot of grief in our family. Especially when it came from people who were very close to us."

"What was difficult for us is that we often knew both sides of the story, the church only one. They judged us on what they knew, not on what they didn't know."

"We set out to be honest about our own struggles toward the elders. But that backfired. We find it hard to trust our leaders since they publicly spoke about what was meant to be kept in the dark."

"Am I doing a good job? That question haunts me. We're all small boys, longing for the 'well done' of a good father."

The pastor's wives, likewise, were very open about their share of grief in the ministry:

"It felt as if the church thought they were getting two full-time workers for the price of one. How on earth can I raise a family, support my husband, and work half a job for free in church? That pressure crushed me in the end."

"My husband and his fellow pastors always say family comes first. But most of them are adulterers. The bride of Christ is more important to them than their own. The shoemaker's son always goes barefoot."

"I often felt caught in the middle. As a pastor's wife, I suffered in silence, as I was unable to play an active role during conflicts. My husband, on the other hand, had the opportunity to reason with people and confront them if necessary. Experiencing the event and the conflict, but having my hands tied behind my back made me feel powerless and vulnerable. For my husband, things were already resolved when I hadn't even gotten to the processing yet".

As she closed her notebook, she was ready to hit the home run. "You do remember James, don't you, Jesus's stepbrother who was stoned because of his faith? Didn't he say that we should count it all joy when we meet trials of various kinds? Apparently, it produces steadfastness. Sounds quite important to me. What about you? There will be no shine without friction, love. It'll take some time for the multitudes to let it all sink in, I'd say, but they will be eating out of your hand in no time, I promise."

I still must figure out a way to get the credit for the wisdom both Marcel and Deborah put forward. I don't want to run the risk that they get all puffed up.

MARCH 2

While having my coffee, I googled Sinead O'Connor's career after the infamous incident in 1992. To put it mildly, it didn't turn out great for her. This increases my doubt toward putting the words *suffering* and *faith* in one sermon at the conference. I put myself at ease by remembering that if I do it and it doesn't end well, I can always blame Marcel and Deborah for the catastrophe. If you play with fire, you can get burned. Worst-case scenario is that both will learn this the hard way.

MARCH 4

How can something feel so good yet be so sad at the same time? After the children went to school this morning and Deborah took her place in front of her class of elementary school children, I decided to take a long walk. Walking helps me to get my thoughts together, and nature has always been my point of contact with God. Here in these Frisian forests, there are plenty of hidden gems where you can feel like you're the only one on earth.

Today was a wonderful winter day. Blue skies, mild winds, and plenty of sunshine. I decided to drive to a newly landscaped park just on the outskirts of town near the canal. While I was driving, I couldn't help but think of Salomé and her parents. I would love to see her back to full strength and health. Preferably after a prayer for healing by me or the elders, but I would also approve of the medical route.

When I walked along the water, that hope was crushed in a million different pieces. I'll explain why, but let me first tell you something about hearing the voice of God. I have been a Christian for about thirty years now and certainly in the early years; I clearly experienced His guidance on the crossroads of life—prophecy, visions, words of knowledge. I've been there and got the T-shirt to prove it.

The last ten years have been a lot quieter on that end. I've more questions than answers to some of the things I've asked and prayed for this last decade. I sometimes think God has moved on to those who do take their spiritual life more seriously than I do. Maybe I've missed a turn somewhere, and he's disappointed with this wayward and stubborn child. I currently trust that I am a privileged person that I believe without seeing. That I'm sure of the things that I cannot feel.

This morning, God decided to show a glimpse of his closeness. I can't explain it, but I know it was Him. When I had finished my first kilometer, I walked a trail that ends at some rocks and a large red buoy that serves as turning and ending point. While I was talking to God about little Salomé, I saw it. It was more of a reality than the ground I was walking on. I saw her. Completely different from what I imagined. My doom image was a little girl with bags under her eyes, covered by tubes in a hospital bed and no hair left to comb. A white blanket trying to keep her fighting and weakening body comfortable. Every parent's nightmare. The nightmare of every sensible person, really.

But what I saw was different. I gazed at her beautiful white dress. Her hair wavy to her shoulders, her skin completely radiant. On her face, a big smile like a child has when she unwraps her anticipated Christmas gift. She was carried by someone, but I couldn't see who it was and where they were going. Her eyes met those of the one who carried her. There was rest, peace, and excitement in her glance as she looked at him. Not a shadow of a doubt or a hint of fear. She trusted him completely.

Then I heard a voice I recognized from my days of old. It was the voice of the Good Shepherd who had called me home three decades ago. "What you've seen, Case, is about to happen. We'll bring her home, and all shall be well." That was it. I broke out in tears for all the right reasons. Because heaven decided to touch earth. Because, if this wasn't a fruit of my imagination, Johan and Marjolein will have to bury their little precious girl. I realized that we could pray, fast, and anoint, but it wouldn't have the outcome we all desired. It shook me to the core.

I'm not prone to tears, but I stayed seated for a short while and waited until the headwind dried them all. I turned around as I made my way back to the parking lot. As I turned around, I saw someone walking the same path toward me. He looked vaguely familiar. Up close I recognized him. "Hey, you're

Salome's grandfather. I saw you playing with her in church last Sunday."

"Nice to meet you, Case. Yes, I enjoyed the service, but I'm not her grandfather. You can call me Granddad if you want, that's fine with me."

Before I get a chance to satisfy my curiosity, he's taken the wheel with no intention of giving it back.

"Case, I need to get something off my chest. Take it to heart or let it be, but every once in a while, Grandpa here receives a message from the Father. At your seminary, they probably would've called it the gift of prophecy or a word of knowledge. Remember when you used to bring presents for your kids when you came home from traveling?"

I did and remembered how happy they were when I opened my suitcase and they saw the gift wrap.

"Bringing a gift was your way of saying that you loved them, right? They experienced your love through the gifts you gave. They're a bit older right now, and they don't need a gift from their father to know that you love them. You've probably been through mountains and valleys together these last years and you pulled through. They know you love them, not because of the presents but because of your presence in all of it.

"Case, that's the way it is in our relationship with God. In those early formative years, it seems like you're receiving multiple back-to-back miracles, answers to prayers, and so on. Those special moments then become memorial stones in your life you can regularly visit to realize God was here and has spoken to me. But the older you get, the more mature you become in Christ, the less the Father gives those kinds of gifts. You should no longer need them, because you have seen that he has been faithful to you for more than thirty years. The Giver is more important than the gift. His presence more important than his presents.

"Well, I hope you appreciate this nugget of wisdom. I must

go. There's a lot on my plate." Without waiting for my reaction, he continued toward the red buoy and the rocks where I sat just minutes ago.

I spent a good amount of time talking to Deborah about what happened this morning. "Honey, how do I tell this to Johan and Marjolein? I can't crush their hopes, can I?"

Deborah replied that I should trust God. "If he spoke to you, I think it's fair to say He can speak to them as well without your interference. Please give it some time."

I am upset that the Omniscient lets me hear the clock strike but doesn't tell me where the clapper hangs, as we say here in Holland.

MARCH 5

I had a bit of a rough night. Couldn't sleep because of what happened yesterday. When I opened my laptop, I found an email from the organizing committee of the Heaven and Earth conference. The subtopic assigned to me is when heaven touches earth. Well... it's a lot better than "worm." I called Marcel this afternoon. He was happy enough with it and thinks it leaves plenty of room to get my out-of-the-ordinary message across.

I'll have to go to Zwolle, though, for a preconference briefing with the other preachers. Kind of looking forward to it. This might be a chance to gently convince them of my out-of-the box ideas for the conference.

This morning we announced in church that we will pray over Salomé and anoint her with oil. Our local flock seemed to be in good spirits. Johan and Marjolein weren't there. Their little girl gets sicker every day. In the open prayer time, we cried out to God to do immeasurably more than all we ask or imagine.

One brother claimed that the devastating spirit of cancer

would leave the small absent body in the name of Jesus. I understood what he meant, but it was cringe worthy at the same time. I value his desire for healing and a miracle to happen. On the other hand, it's so pretentious to put everything in these neat spiritual categories that we've designed.

As his words blared through our sanctuary, some of my sheep shrank. Some had overcome the same disease, others had to take a dear one to the grave because of the destruction it wreaked. I could hear them think: "Was it really a spirit of cancer that crushed my dear mother? But she walked so close to the Lord. Why didn't that spirit leave her when we, me and my brother, prayed over her? Wasn't my faith strong enough? Did God shake his head and say: 'Ye of little faith, if only your prayer was more powerfully, I would've healed her.'"

I talked to my zealous brother after the service. He promised he would choose his words more carefully next time. It is difficult to know what's right or wrong in these open prayer times. You don't want to set too many boundaries. But you don't want it to spin out of control like the bamboo in your backyard.

MARCH 9

Tonight was the night. Two elders and I headed over to the Boersma family to pray over Salomé and anoint her with oil. I've received countless text messages from church members that made it crystal clear that we were not the only ones praying tonight. I can only be thankful for these Frisian Baptists who are both down to earth and full of faith. Their focus is on the heavenly things, but they have both feet firmly on the ground.

One of my fellow elders had the jitters. This was his first time. I assured him it's not rocket science. "When you have a rock-solid faith in God and in the fact that He's well able to heal but sometimes chooses differently, you'll be fine, Reinder. Just be yourself. The church didn't put your name forward for eldership without reason. You're doing a great job so far."

Reinder is in his mid-thirties, a father to four, and gifted with a great sense of responsibility. Although this is an obvious recipe for compassion fatigue, his gentle and loving spirit balances everything well.

We cycled toward the Boersma residence, not speaking much along the way. We looked like a bunch of football players gathered in Anfields' player tunnel just before a massive game. We had our eyes on the prize. We all prepared in our own way. One had taken a long walk, the other had taken time off work to spend some time reading Scripture and fasting. Around six o'clock, because we knew the little one needed her rest, I rang the bell. I couldn't help but think about what happened in the park the other day, despite trying to put it out of mind.

"Come on in guys, it's warmer inside than where you are standing. Great to see you." Johan seemed less tense than we were. Marjolein took our coats as we settled into the sofa in the TV room. The little one frolicked through the room and played with a necklace with a few colored beads. "She got it at the hospital earlier this week. It's called a Rainbow Trail. Each bead tells a story. She got the little yellow ball for a scan; the purple butterfly was added after a bone marrow puncture, and the smiley she received after getting her first chemo. She feels like a princess wearing it. Don't you think she looks gorgeous, pastor?" Marjolein said.

Little Salomé was looking at me, eagerly expecting my positive response. "Oh Salomé, can I try it on for a moment? It's amazing. I don't think I've ever seen such a beautiful necklace in my whole life."

Her eyes were as big as saucers as she jumped onto my lap and put the necklace around my neck.

"Will you help Mom and Dad remember to have me take it

off before I leave? If I take it with me, I'm sure Deborah would want it for keeps."

She smiled and looked at Daddy, who assured her that I won't leave without giving the necklace back.

We spent a couple of minutes on table talk, but then it was time for prayer. Reinder encouraged us all that what we were about to do was within God's will for us and his church. He opened his Bible and read a part of James 5:

Is anyone among you sick? Let him call to the elders of the church and let them pray over him, anointing him with oil in the name of the Lord. (James 5:14 ESV)

He continued, affirming that the prayer of the righteous person has great power. Elijah was a man just like us and he prayed fervently that it might not rain and so it happened. Then he prayed again, and the floodgates of heaven opened wide. How wonderful it is it to be in a room with like-minded people, being in one accord.

"Pastor, is it possible to sing a song together before we pray?" Marjolein asked.

Over the years, I have sung many songs at times like this. Many of them were old hymns, a treasured memory for those coming to age in the winter of their lives.

"Salomé likes to sing and dance to a kid's praise song. But maybe that's a bit awkward for such a time as this?"

I assured her that it was no such thing but warned her that I would not be dancing as to not upset the heavenlies. We laughed and sang, Salomé our little worship leader. Especially the second verse touched our hearts, and we found it hard to keep the tears in:

He cares for all the sick children
He knows their needs and their pain
Yes for all the big and small ones
He'll give power to sustain

The only one who could finish without crying was Salomé.

Her confidence seemed to surpass ours. Believe like a child. It was a song of thanksgiving, and together we praised God for being our Lord and Helper in times of need.

The necklace was still around my neck. For a moment, I carried her sickness on my shoulders. I looked forward to the day there will be no more Rainbow Trails, that they are considered a thing from the past, from a world that's gone and has been renewed.

The little girl sat on Johan's lap. Our hands were filled with a little bit of olive oil and each in turn we prayed our prayer of faith. We pleaded with God as if her and our lives depended on it, but we knew that wasn't the case.

Her life was not in human frail hands like ours but in the perfect hands of a loving Father. I realized that prayer gave strength to bear but would not lead to her healing. Or did I misinterpret His voice? In a moment of nagging self-doubt, I opened my eyes and noticed we had a visitor. It was Grandpa. He was sitting in the same chair where I sat a while ago when the Boersmas told me the devastating news, next to the pellet stove in the conservatory. He seemed relaxed, in control. He held a finger to his lips as a gesture of silence. This wasn't the time to ask questions. We needed to continue with what we were doing.

After fifteen minutes or so, we ended our time of prayer. Salomé had lifted herself in her pajamas, ready to go to bed. But not before I'd taken off the necklace and had given it back to her. She went to sleep, and we decided to cast all our burdens to the Lord, for we know He cares for us.

MARCH 13

It could've been a perfectly normal Sunday today were it not for our sound technician having a complete off day. This led to a lot of hilariousness among everyone with a bad sense of humor, a limited sense of responsibility, and stagnating spiritual growth. Today was one of those days where you know that there's still a lot of work to be done.

Today my Pentecostal brother Henry van Oostrum came to Zwagerheide to open the Word. Perhaps his nickname "Father Henry" rings a bell. We had a great time in Ireland together, that's for sure. Henry is always willing to answer for the hope that is in him and willing to arrive in the wrong place at the wrong time. He was supposed to come down four weeks ago, but he had to cancel because he was taken into custody. He gave me a call in the middle of the night: "Case, I'm incarcerated, but I'm innocent, not sure I'm going to make it, okay? Pray for me. Love, Henry!"

I preached that morning, as he was nowhere to be found. I went to the county jail later that day and found he had been arrested during a "gender reveal party." To cut a long story short, He turned up naked to reveal his gender, a clear misinterpretation of the nature of such a party. Forgiving Baptists that we are, we decided to give him another chance to come and preach.

He turned up late, and there was little time left to pray together before the service would start. After praying, he quickly went to our sound technician, who pinned a wireless microphone to his jacket.

I nestled myself in at the back of the church, writing down some sermon ideas for the Heaven on Earth conference. Then things went sideways. The technician accidentally had Henry's microphone on when it was supposed to be muted. This happened to me one time, preaching in the city of Leeuwarden.

After the service, the organ player approached me. "Brother Parker, you are a decent preacher but a horrible singer." When I listened to the service later that week, it turned out that my microphone wasn't only recording my preaching but also my singing, and I had to agree with the old man.

What happened to Father Henry today was a bit more consequential. In my first book, I informed you of Henry's bladder problems and his snoring. Today we found out he probably also suffers from irritable bowel syndrome. His late arrival, plus the fact that this was his first time in Zwagerheide and preaching to Baptists, apparently caused so much stress that his intestines began to rebel against him.

Because his microphone was still switched on, we could hear his small little footsteps on our marble floor in the hallway. They were easy to recognize, for Henry has a limp.

Due to his full, gray beard, he was asked to play Santa Claus for the children in his hometown. They thought it would be fun to put Santa on a horse called Hysterical Friction, but it didn't go as planned. Father Henry fell and broke his hip, a limp as a permanent reminder.

As he walked through the hallway this morning, it sounded as if someone was zipping open a tent. We fervently hoped he was going to do a number one, but unfortunately that was far from the truth.

In surround sound, all seventy souls present heard a live recording of Henry's visit to the men's room. At the first bang we thought of a short circuit at the mixer, but soon different, unheard sounds came through our loudspeakers. It was like listening to one of those radio plays from back in the days, and it only lasted thirty seconds. The first bang was followed by the sound of a ram's horn, and then it seemed as if five or six obese teenagers fell in a pool after a quick ride on a slide that was too steep. Their water fun ended with what looked like some soft tones coming from a tuba and a sigh of relief from the one playing it.

We were shocked and didn't know what to do as we could hear his footsteps coming back to the sanctuary. When he entered the church hall, completely ignorant of what had just happened, a few of our teenagers started to giggle. When he welcomed us all and said that his theme for today was "Forgetting those things that are behind," no one could stop laughing.

I prayed that nothing like this would happen next week at our "everyone gets to play" church service. It's probably spiritual warfare. Well, I'm not having it. It was at least great to see Johan and Marjolein having a laugh during the incident.

MARCH 15

Marcel sent a story this morning, and it got me thinking about the conference again. It has been attributed to an Irish clergyman. I can't get it out of my head. Maybe putting it down in writing will help. It might be a good one to share during my sermon.

* * *

There once was an old Irish saint who lived on Achill Island. Well, saint. He used to be a devout Catholic, but a lot had happened along the way. He wouldn't go to mass regularly and would've described himself as a CEO Christian: Christmas and Easter Only. But as the years went by, there was no desire to go to St. Thomas's church, even around the holidays.

He and his parents visited another church when he was just a child, but there was nothing left at the site but one stone wall where the ravens built their nest. You could say that his weakening faith and the deterioration of the building went hand in hand.

After a short and unpleasant conversation with an oncologist at Mayo University Hospital, it had become clear to him that he had to go the way of this earth. At the time of year, where the days were getting shorter and the nights longer, his life had the same fate.

On a windy Monday morning, he went to St. Thomas's church looking for the parish priest. After a few minutes, they met at the altar. "Father, I won't beat around the bush. I am going to face a time of suffering, which will lead to my departure. Amid this misery, I have started my quest for my faith from the past. You may think I'm a hypocrite, but I can't be very bothered with that at this stage of life, if you don't mind."

The priest looked at the old man and concluded that God had probably already started a work in him. This was the next phase. "Now tell me this, sir; are you looking for God or have you found him already?"

The old man smiled and answered, tongue in cheek, "Well, the man upstairs is hard to find, compared to his representative on Achill Island. I've reengineered my life for the last couple of weeks, dug into my past, but haven't found him so far. I could call Him the Great Absentee. Are you shocked by that, Father?"

The priest urged him to sit and poured him a cup of tea. "May I ask how long you have left?"

"Certainly, Father. The oncologist said a few weeks to a month at best."

The priest looked through the stained-glass windows and put his hand on the man's shoulder. "In that case, there is not much I can do for you. But I think you will be helped by making a small adjustment in your bedroom. Would you be open to that?"

The man looked at the priest as if he had just asked him to eat some magic mushrooms as medicine for his disease.

"No, I'm serious. I would like you to do just one thing, as I'm sure it will help you to realize He is not absent, but present. I would like you to put a chair next to your bed. Do you think that's possible?"

The old man said that he owned three chairs, and he had no problem putting one next to the bed.

"Will you come around every day to sit on that chair, Father, and read the Scriptures with me?"

"No, I won't. That chair belongs to Christ. I want you to imagine that Christ Himself is coming to meet with you, sitting on that chair. You'll find that He's a real friend, closer than a brother."

"Well, Father, they say that the proof of the pudding is in the eating." The old man promised to give it a try and shook the priest's hand for the first and the last time in his life.

Two weeks later, the priest was called by the man's son. "Father, we want to let you know that our father died last night. We found your number in his notebook and thought he might have discussed his last wishes with you. Would you like to come over?"

The priest consented and headed for the old cottage in one of the most remote areas of Achill. Upon arrival, the son took him aside. "There was something strange when we found my father last night."

The priest invited him to continue.

"Well, you see. For the last four days, our father was unable to get up out of bed, and me and my sisters stopped by every few hours to supply hospice care for him. When I came by last night and opened the door to his bedroom, I found him in bed. I checked his breathing, and he had passed away, but there was something odd. His head was not on the pillow, but on the chair next to him. What do you make of that, Father?"

The priest remained silent but knew that heaven had touched earth without anyone ever knowing about it. The old man knocked, and the door was opened for him.

MARCH 17

Everyone is in bed. Technically, it's March 18 already, please forgive me. I was working in the local library this afternoon when I stumbled upon a short poem by John Oxenham.

To every man there openeth
A way, and ways, and a way,
And the high soul climbs the highway,
And the low soul gropes the low,
And in between, on the misty flats,
The rest drift to and fro.
But to every man there openeth
A highway, and a low.
And every man decideth
The way his soul shall go.

It felt like the Lord impressing it upon my heart (not even sure if I'm allowed to say that as a Baptist!) that most Christians are satisfied if they do not or do no longer walk the low road. They have no criminal record; they don't take drugs or other prohibited substances. They have no sky-high debt and don't live life in the fast lane. They are not found in the brothels of the city or the pubs in the village. They live a very respectful and well-ordered life. They think they are on the right track.

But I wonder how many of them ever reach the highways. Where there is radical discipleship. Where there is obedience. Where the rubber hits the road. The way of self-denial, crucifying the flesh and all its lust. Where you value others higher than yourself. Where we read the road signs, time and time again: You are crucified, dead and buried, so live accordingly. Let My will be done and not yours. In the way you speak, act, behave. In the things you lay down and take up. In your silence, in your coming and going, in your sitting and standing. On that high road, you will find the altar where you offer yourself daily as a sacrifice.

The devastating result of leaving the low road but never entering the high one is that you'll float amid the misty plains. You are in no man's land. Where there is no victory over besetting sin due to lack of spiritual zeal. Where time and money are given but never to the extent that it will cost you. Where the ego is always revived. Where we call out, "Lord, here I am, send him!" Where the treasure on earth surpasses the treasure in heaven. In those misty plains, pride and selfish ambition get the better of humility and dedication. Where "I surrender all" is sung but never practiced.

How many of us live on those misty plains of glooming half-heartedness, not sure whom to serve? The frustrating thing with mist is that it takes away your view of what is higher than yourself.

I remember one trip during our retreat last year. Cornelius and Eileen took us to the Comeragh Mountains where the counties of Waterford and Cork intersect. It had to be a memorable moment, but the mist threw a wrench in the works. Instead of waterfalls, coastlines, and uninterrupted views of fifty shades of green, we couldn't see a thing and were glad we could avoid a collision with some stray sheep! That is what mist does; it deprives you of the view of beautiful reality. This is also true for spiritual mediocrity.

I was over the moon with myself for reaching these lofty conclusions. I don't think the visitors were aware of what genius was working on his sermon on the second floor today. Good night.

March 18

Two more days until our "everyone gets to play" church service. I have not yet received a cancellation from my uncle Vincent, very pleased with that. The first act that day will be from Br. Baumgart, one of those rare Baptists who is the touchy-feely kind of person. He's a great lad, though a bit strange. Especially if you compare him to other Frisians. He respects authority; I like that. Which is why he already sent an email to tell us about his act.

* * *

Dear Brethren,

I feel compelled to tell you about my performance next Sunday. I believe it was the Holy Spirit himself who was leading you during our last brainstorm. I noticed that you no longer want to get in His way through micromanaging our services. God only knows how you have limited Him in recent years, right? But enough about that.

The reason I want to play my part is completely outside of me. I received an unction straight from the heavenlies. Last week I chopped my superfoods and watched an episode of The Sand Magician. *That man brought Bible stories to life using sand and a projector; it was amazing, brethren!*

When I looked at my superfoods again, I was amazed to see that the macaroni I had just thrown into a pan was now back on the counter...in the shape of a cross! I then said to my Siamese cat, "Cuby, what if I can do with macaroni what that handsome red curly haired brother can do with sand? What if I'm called to be... the macaroni magician!"

The striking thing was that Cuby did something he never does. He jumped unto the countertop and sat down next to the macaroni and closed his eyes. It looked as if he had some kind of halo on his head, but maybe that was the built-in LED ceiling lights. Who knows, right? To be on the safe side, I decided to subject the word macaroni *to a solid word study, like biblical scholars do. After a few seconds on Google, I found that "Maca" is also a superfood. It's known for increasing your libido and producing a fertility increasing effect. It felt as if heaven told me, "Baumgart, your act will be incredibly fruitful."*

I've gone into hiding until next Sunday. The spiritual warfare is intense. I can therefore no longer be in the public eye. The opponent will do everything in his power to break through the heavenly defense line to get to me. He might try to throw me before a bus or worse, hit me with a stomach bug! But don't worry, not all is lost. There is plenty of food in the house. I have prepped for lots worse than this. Please pray for a hedge of protection and all other good hedges you might think of.

Blessings, a brotherly kiss,

Br. Baumgart

* * *

The Macaroni Magician. Perhaps this service will bring forth our first celebrity. Will this be the start of Baumgart's career or the demise of our congregation? I've decided to tear these pages out of my diary if things go horribly wrong. Government documents, state secrets, and brilliant diaries like this have one thing in common. When they are harmful to the writer, it is important to choose confidentiality over transparency.

MARCH 20

I don't think I've felt so humiliated before. My career is over. All is lost. The panic attack is gone, so I'd better tell you what happened earlier.

When I picked up Uncle Vincent this morning, I smelled the familiar scent of cigars, alcohol, and cheap perfume. I tried to mask it by overdosing him on peppermint. Once we arrived at the church, we were warmly received by our welcoming team consisting of two—objectively spoken—good-looking blondes. Uncle mumbled something about curves and that watching is something other than touching, but I decided to not go into it and escorted him to the front row because we were already late.

The church was packed. Many locals came, and brother van Beelen, the driving force behind it all, almost floated toward the stage to welcome us. The first act came from Br. Baumgart. I felt my heart skip slightly when van Beelen rolled an old slide projector to the stage while Baumgart himself dragged an XXL package of macaroni to the platform. Cuby also joined him for the occasion.

Call it stage fright or spiritual warfare, but the bag tore, and ten kilograms of macaroni hit the glass plate of the projector, shattering it to pieces.

In retrospect, I would have given my life to help Baumgart resume his act at all costs, but I didn't. That let the genie out of the bottle. It caused a vacuum in the program, and if there's one thing you don't want with Vincent around, it is a vacuum. Before I knew it, he slipped through my fingers toward the microphone, and I knew what was coming. I prayed earnestly for Armageddon, the second coming, and the bears who consumed children when they scolded Elisha. My prayers weren't answered.

Uncle Vincent used to be a stand-up comedian, quite a famous one. The only problem is that most of his jokes involve material that is not quite suited for church. It's impossible to laugh at these obscenities as a shepherd, at least not publicly. I came under the impression that my parishioners were in for a treat, but one I'd rather spare them from.

"Hello, you lot. Is this turned on or what? Are we having a good time? You probably know me as Uncle Vincent, the evangelization project of your chief. Unfortunately, still without any result. That should make you think: A pastor who can't even convert his uncle, can you still take him seriously?"

My blood ran cold. This alone was enough to make the angels weep.

"Let's lighten up the place a little bit. Who can tell the difference between a car tire and thrity-six used condoms?" Vincent waved the microphone towards the horrified crowd as an invitation for answers. Even the unbelievers among us were silent. You could hear a pin drop. "Well, one is a good year, the other is a great year!"

No one laughed... except Vincent. His eyes were fiery; he had the momentum going. "Hey, you... pretty girl in the third row. Thanks for welcoming me at the door. You look lovely. How much did you pay for those pants, if I may ask?"

One of our newer members, Priscilla, reluctantly answered that she got them at a discount for $20.

"Well, if you come over to my place afterwards you can get them 100 percent off!"

I stared at Vincent and made a throat slashing sign, hoping he would stop. He looked at me and whispered that everything was going to be alright. I wasn't convinced and started to consider other career options... like flipping burgers in a fast-food restaurant... four thousand miles away. Under a false name and with some plastic surgery, just to be sure.

"Just kidding people. This was only a test to see if you are holy people. No one laughed, that's a good sign. I can see you're changed. I respect that." Uncle Vincent continued like nothing had happened. "I've got one more thing for you guys, and then I'll call it quits. I have a favor to ask. I'm having some trouble with my prosthetic eye."

I've noticed that there was grace for Vincent among my people. They wanted to give him a second chance and would like to pray for him. I wasn't so sure.

"Last week I had a serious incident with my prosthetic eyeball. I always put it in a glass of lukewarm water when I go to bed for safety reasons. After drinking too much the other day, I reached for the glass next to my bed but got the wrong one. I accidentally drank the glass with my eyeball in it."

I saw several of my flock try to empathize with a boozy man who had just drunk his own eyeball.

"So, the next day, I went to my doctor to explain what had happened. He was very honest about the remedy. 'Mr. Parker, if you're going to make an exculpatory statement after drinking your first cup of coffee this morning, the eye will come out again, I'm sure.' I wasn't at all reassured and said to him, 'Doctor, could you maybe have a look and see if my eyeball is already showing up between my buttocks? Or is that too much of an ask on an early Monday morning?' Fortunately, he was okay with it and started the investigation. When I was standing before him, I was surprised when he said, 'Mr. Parker, I don't see anything at all.' To which I said, in a bent-over position, 'That's funny doctor, because I can see you!'"

There were a few immature believers and some unbelievers who almost fell from their seats, laughing. I made a note to invite them for our next Christianity Explored course. Uncle Vincent was on a winning streak without any intention of stopping. He approached one of our older congregants, Sister Wiersma. He bent to her eye and whispered that he had a finger cramp and asked if she was willing to pull his finger to relieve him from the pain. I saw Vincent moving the microphone to this bottom, and I knew what was about to happen. Fortunately, our sound engineer had his head screwed on the right way today and lowered the volume to zero. I found strength to walk up to him and asked him to sit down and be quiet for the rest of the service.

When we left the sanctuary afterwards, he tried to get Priscilla's phone number, without any success. He told me he thoroughly enjoyed himself and complimented me on the fact that we were open-minded enough to give him the stage for a few minutes. After enjoying his beer-braised beef short ribs, as a reward for his contribution, I decided to drop him off with Gizmo and Gremlin a little earlier than predicted.

MARCH 21

I'm not so sure this diary will be a blessing for the next generations. Today I chose to keep the curtains closed in my office. I came across some excellent job openings. Deborah said that I should not always look for greener grass at the slightest setback. I'm convinced that when one door shuts, he will open another one.

MARCH 22

One of these job openings has me mesmerized. I feel led to think that God has something else for me in store. I showed it to Marcel this afternoon. He urged me to stay put, "The grass isn't always greener on the other side, Case."

MARCH 23

I had difficulties falling asleep tonight. I can't think of anything but a possible career switch. It isn't every day that once-in-a-lifetime opportunities present themselves. Father Henry called me this morning saying he received a vision. The bottom line was that the grass isn't always greener on the other side.

It's so confusing. I wish God would just make it clear what He wants me to do. It is inhumane to be tossed back and forth like this.

MARCH 24

I've decided to stay in Zwagerheide. A rolling stone gathers no moss, they say. No cross, no crown. No blessing without a struggle. I'm not out of the woods yet, but I believe there is a task ahead, the journey has just started and all that. It was probably Satan trying to lure me away because of my incredible fruitfulness over here. When he gets uneasy, he tries to persuade you to find greener grass. Well, it's not going to happen with me. I'm stronger than that. Sunday was a bit turbulent, but nothing can stop me.

This change of thought may also have something to do with our church archives. In a filing cabinet, I found the rejected evangelization ideas from previous years. If you read it, our "everyone gets to play" service wasn't too bad. Call it quirky, radical, or utterly stupid, but these out-of-the-box ideas apparently originated somewhere in the twilight zone of bewilderment and divine guidance amid our flock in recent years. I've included the reports of my predecessors, reflecting on their own brainstorm sessions.

1. Church member rocket launch: REJECTED 2018

"It's from the Lord, he confirmed it," Brother van Nes proclaimed. "After a few drinks with the lads at the darts club, I got a fantastic idea on the way back that will raise the profile of our church. Brethren, to infinity and beyond! With God's help, we will be the first Baptists ever to go into space! My proposal is that we will get one or two elders and baptismal candidates to conduct the first baptism service in the galaxy."

While van Nes was still speaking, I beckoned someone from the pastoral care team to chat with Mr. and Mrs. van Nes about his growing alcohol problem. I hope they don't ask too many questions. I'm at the same darts club that he is.

Van Nes was beyond himself and the handkerchief, which Sister Visser supplied to dab the foam off his lips, was not up for the challenge. "Once there, we can take our banner with the church logo and contact details and plant it on the moon next to Neil Armstrong's US flag! Maybe our technical people can arrange a livestream so we can watch it live?!"

Let's be perfectly honest. The opportunity dawned on me that this was my chance to increase my own comfort. I had one conflict-ridden elder in mind whom I would send into orbit without thinking twice. Wouldn't it be delightful to say, "Houston, we just solved a problem" while launching him sky bound in a hastily prepared rocket?

My dream was shattered by Sister Vanderbilt. "Brethren, don't you know that our Lord said that we will be his witnesses in Jerusalem, Judea, and Samaria and to the end of the earth? He didn't mention the galaxy, so we should refrain from this wicked gesture of van Nes.

Br. Van Nes was wondering whether he had misunderstood God's voice as he walked away from the whiteboard.

Yours truly, Pastor van Barneveld, brainstorm session 2018.

2. The assembly of the conspiracy theorist of the latter-day Baptists: REJECTED 2016

Tonight's final thought came about after too many people shouted toward the stage at the same time. You could compare those few minutes to some kind of silent disco. Everyone heard something different and was dancing to their own beat. One murmured something about a symposium on Baptist conspiracy theories. The other wondered if polygamy would make the church more attractive. Yet another wanted to set up a class to practice the rapture (from a premillennial pretribulationistic perspective) together. "It is such an important theme in the Bible, shouldn't we be prepared? Let's try and undress simultaneously and leave our clothes on the floor. Let's start our cars without getting in. Others can practice how to disappear in a large group of people without anyone noticing."

Brother Balker had seen enough. Somewhat cynical, he summed up the craziness with the proposal to change the name of the church to the Assembly of Conspiracy Theorists of the Latter-day Baptists. Some gave him the silent treatment during our break time, but I believe he saved us from a whole lot of trouble. I wonder if evangelism should really be so complicated, or if you can just life your life with Christ in a world that's looking for the answers that the Gospel provides: Acceptance, forgiveness, amazing grace.

Yours truly, Pastor Smit, 2016.

APRIL 3

I try to take Saturdays off. Many of my colleagues are still busy with their sermons one day before, but I try to avoid it. If you come to think of it, our job is quite unusual. On the one hand, we have loads of freedom. For example, I don't have to get up at five in the morning like Johan to go to a building site. I don't do night shifts either, like some of my parishioners who are working down in the factory. No manager will ask me what I did yesterday, what I'm going to do today, or what the obstacles are for tomorrow.

On the other hand, I never sign out. My van never comes back from the building site, and no one will invite me for a drink after working hours. Those who aspire to be a pastor should know that they'll have a great deal of flexibility, but they must be available around the clock.

This morning Johan called asking if I could stop by. I could tell from the tone of his voice that it couldn't wait. This was a no-brainer, even on my day off. I gave Deborah a kiss, put on my walking shoes, and headed over to the Boersmas.

"Thank you for coming, Pastor. We appreciate you dropping by at such short notice." I could feel the tension in the air, an emotional lava that slowly breaks through the strata of the earth, seeking its way out.

"No bother, Marjolein, I'm here to help and listen." I couldn't hear Salomé singing. As I walked in, I saw her lying on the couch underneath an electric blanket. Her skin was pale, her eyes closed. Her Rainbow Trail necklace was on the table. It was longer than the first time I saw it, which explained why her head was bald. There was a bucket next to the couch, as the sickness was getting worse. Chemo is like a bad gardener. It not only pulls the weeds but at the same time also your newly planted rhododendron and the lawn you just laid.

"Br. Parker, we had a long meeting with the pediatric oncologist yesterday. Two things appeared from the latest scan and the blood results. The first thing is that our girl is getting weaker by the day. The second thing is that she won't heal. They are willing to continue treatment, so she might be with us for a couple of months, but that's it. The oncologist's advice was to stop treatment. He's afraid that the medicine itself will cause her death and not the cancer.

"We decided to stop the treatment when they promised to do everything in their power to make her feel as comfortable as they can. Pastor, this is the hardest decision we ever made in our lives." Marjolein's voice broke, and Johan swallowed his tears.

I imagined myself being in their shoes as I thought back to the time my kids were Salomé's age. Would I have been as strong as they are? Would I have cursed heaven, burned my Bible, and resorted to some other deity?

I recently read an article on suffering, and it included a conversation between Corrie ten Boom and her father, Casper. Corrie told her father that she was afraid that she would not be able to stand if she ever was persecuted for her faith. Father ten Boom urged Corrie to sit with him for a moment. "Honey, if you must take the train from Haarlem to Amsterdam, when will I give you the money to buy a train ticket? Do I do that four weeks in advance or on the day you need it?"

"On the day I travel." Corrie answered.

"It's the same with the things you worry about, love. There will be strength at the appointed time. The power you need for tomorrow won't be provided today."

"Johan, Marjolein. I'm not sure what to say. How can I help you?" Again I feel way out of my league.

"Your presence, crying, and praying is enough, Pastor. We were up all night and talked through the different scenarios. We would like you to conduct her funeral if that day comes. Would you be open for that?"

"Of course, I will cancel everything if I need to."

We spent some time in prayer. I looked at the little frail girl on the couch; she was bald but beautiful and on her way to glory.

Just when I was about to leave, Johan took the floor. "Something strange happened yesterday, before we had to go to the hospital. When I had cleaned up my tools at two o'clock and planned to drive home, a stranger stood in front of me. He looked friendly but also a bit sad. He came even closer and put his hand on my shoulders and said only three words before he left. There was something familiar about him, but I'm sure it was the first time I saw him. Isn't that strange, Pastor?"

I was about to agree, but then I recalled my meetings with Grandpa, which were a bit odd to say the least. "So, what did he say, Johan?"

"The only thing he said was, 'He knows, Johan.'"

"So have you asked him what he meant by that?" I've always found it a challenge to hide my curiosity.

"I didn't need to, Br. Parker. I knew exactly what he meant; I'll tell you why. The last few weeks, I have had a hard time falling asleep because of all the sorrow in this house. I am a bit of an introvert; words don't come easy to me. But I can pray. My prayers are short, nothing compared to yours, but I don't think that matters too much as long as they're genuine and straight from the heart. When Marjolein is fast asleep and I'm lying there, staring up at the ceiling, I sometimes get up and go up to Salomé's bedroom. I just sit there, looking at her, praying over her.

"But this week, I looked out through her window and saw the full moon, the stars, and maybe even a planet or two. I looked at them and realized that God made all this and holds the world in His hands. I opened the window and felt the cold wind blowing in my face. I said my prayer for that night, which were only three words: You know, Lord. So, when that man spoke those three words, two days later, I knew exactly what he meant, although I still don't understand how he knew about my prayer. But some things may not be for us to know, I guess, right?"

I was about to leave, but decided to take them up on the offer for a cup of coffee. As we are talking about Johan's experience, Marjolein suddenly bursts out in laughing. "I probably shouldn't with everything that's going on, Pastor, but your uncle Vincent is some man. He seems a little far from the Kingdom, but he can tell a joke and work a crowd, that's for sure. Our cell group offered a meal to Br. Baumgart, by the way, to ease the hurt a little bit. Johan told me to cook him macaroni and cheese, but Baumgart refused."

It was time to leave. Maybe I'll take Monday off instead. I'll be preaching in Veenendaal tomorrow at one of those emerging church plants. Blowing some dust off an old sermon will probably do the trick.

April 4

Some truths are better left unspoken. That was my thought after reading the bulletin of the church I preached at this morning. It was printed in cost-effective gray and included a crossword puzzle, a drawing for the kids, and the outcome of a vote they did on installing a new heating system. But what really stood out for me was their ground-breaking way of caring for each other's burdens. They had decided to not only mention the ailment but also how it came about. I must tell you this produced some interesting reading material. I knew straightaway that a copy should be included in this wondrous diary. Here we go.

* * *

Dear members,

This is your pastoral team speaking. Here you'll find the abrupt, short-lived, relapsed, and long-term sufferers of our flock. Most of them would appreciate a greeting card from your end, others don't have a clue what to do with all those poorly written postcards. We pray a spirit of discernment over you, so you know who to write and who not to write. Here's what we got in this week. Please lift them up in prayer!

Brother **John van Bimsbergen (58)** took a fall this week and tore off his Achilles tendon.

Bareld and his wife Dini were at the local shopping center when all toilets turned out to be closed. Bareld hurried outside and started panicking. He noticed the bushes behind the parking lot and made his way to do a number two. In a squatting position, he suddenly noticed a large dog approaching. Dini claimed afterwards that it looked more like a wolf or jackal. We are still not sure. Anyway, Bareld fled but did not get far as his trousers were still on his ankles, causing him to trip on the edge of the shrubbery tearing his tendon. We wish him all the best and a speedy recovery!

Brother **Jan van Koningsveld (35)** spent some time at the hospital yesterday evening due to heart rhythm disorder.

As you know, last week Jan's son Damian was baptized. What you probably don't know is that he is quite a successful practical joker, with his own YouTube channel. Last night he decided to prank his father. He waited for him to come home as he hid in the dumpster, wearing a horror clown mask. When poor Jan came home, Damian jumped out, screaming. Jan was so fascinated by all of this that the adrenaline rushed through his veins at such a speed that he was briefly unconscious. After fourteen minutes, he regained consciousness, but his heart was still all over the place. They did a great job in the hospital. They stopped the heart and shocked it back in its original rhythm. Damian is still editing the material; it should be online after the service for all of you to enjoy.

Brother **Arie de Vries (89)** suffers from a broken vertebra after falling from a ladder.

You might be aware of a new ultramodern wellness that has recently opened its doors next to Arie and Johanna's farm, on the outskirts of Veenendaal. During his weekly poker night Arie overheard some of his mates saying that, during dusk, there's a lot of incoming and outgoing traffic near the outdoor saunas. Determined to crush this kind of unholy gossip, Arie took his extendable ladder and high-definition camera to see it with his own eyes. Unfortunately, some of the scarcely dressed ladies on the other side of Arie's laurel hedges started screaming when his auto flash went off. The shouting introduced him to the laws of gravity as he fell and landed on his tailbone. We are looking for some volunteers to cook Arie a meal as Johanna has left the farm angry. Some would claim that Arie's intentions surrounding this photography session weren't at all Christian. That he made his bed and that he should lie on it. Johanna is one of them. The elders will be at the crime scene tomorrow, interrogating Arie to find out what really happened last Thursday.

Sister **Tammy Jansen (28)** broke both of her legs.

During the last cell group of the season, Tini stayed a little longer than needed. Although we have already urged John and Dini, their cell group leaders, to cut off the alcohol during prayer meetings they still are rebellious toward the elders. One of the neighbors called us to say that Tini and her boyfriend Ad were causing a row outside before they cycled home. Sadly,

Tini's estimation of the viaduct proved to be wrong, and she tumbled down. The good thing was that her high alcohol levels numbed the otherwise excruciating pain she suffered from breaking two legs at the same time. Please remove everything from your fruit baskets that may ferment or that could be used to brew your own alcoholic drinks.

Thanks for praying. If you hear anything interesting, please send it along to us for next week's church bulletin.

APRIL 5

Monday is the most difficult and discouraging day of the week for most pastors, and it's the day they need the most encouragement and replenishment. Having said that, I'd stopped taking Mondays off years ago. You are the worst version of yourself, and you should keep that as far away from your wife and children as possible. Why is a pastor exhausted on Monday, you might wonder? Well, here are four reasons:

1. He has preached two or three times for different groups. Research has shown that half an hour of intensive preaching is equal to twenty hours of labor. I can't reveal the source; if it proves to be fake news that wouldn't be convenient.
2. He spent most of the day talking to a great variety of people. Especially for introverts like me, that is an agony. Some received a vision that they want to share, others think the music was too loud or that there wasn't enough parking space at church. They often think they're the only ones wanting a quick word with their pastor. I'll tell you this; they're not.
3. While he preaches, he scans the room, and he sees people missing. His eyes go back and forth over the sanctuary, and he wonders where they are. Is it his

preaching or the sermon series? Did they fall out
with other brothers and sisters? Is that emerging
church down the corner involved in sheep stealing?

4. The adrenaline levels are still high after coming
   home dead tired. It only takes one little spark to set
   him on fire. Bad table manners, a toddler's scream
   or a rebellious sigh from a teenager rolling his eyes.
   The under shepherd finds it hard to control himself
   and wonders if he is even fit for the ministry, being
   short-tempered like he is. When his wife states the
   obvious about being kind and gentle in church but
   a monster at home, that seals the deal for him. It's
   time to quit. My suggestion is to avoid eye contact
   with every pastor until two hours after the sermon.

So, now you know why pastors shouldn't take Mondays off.
If you're reading this and are preparing for ministry. Do some
administration, emails, long walks instead and make sure you
drink a good cup of coffee while doing it.

APRIL 9

During my nap this afternoon, I received a terrifying vision.
Maybe because I was contemplating what Bible translation I'm
going to use for the conference.

I was teleported to the year 2035. I found myself in the
department of innovation and strategy of the Dutch-Belgian
Bible Society. A group of people had just finished an hour-long
brainstorm session. They were sweating, giving each other high-
fives and clearly happy with the progress they made: Four new
Bibles were about to see the light of day. Hidden behind the
mobile air conditioner, I was introduced to four new
showpieces that will be used for the Christianization of our
nations. I'll entrust this to my diary as a warning. If it may come

to pass, I'll be considered a prophet. That will look awfully good on my resume. Especially if I decide to apply for a job with the Pentecostals if the Baptists end up wanting to get rid of me.

THE VEGAN BIBLE

The Message Bible with some animal-friendly adaptations. For example, the passages around animal sacrifices have been edited. In this edition, only salads, soy burgers, peas, and lentils will be offered for reconciliation. The people of Israel will be supplied with flying cauliflower and tacos with curtido and jalapeno sauce while making their way through the desert. With the VeganBible, the selection committee will spare no effort to eliminate reverse vegetarianism. For example, Jonah will not travel in the inside of the fish but clings to an orca's pectoral fin as he travels back to Tel Aviv, and the lions' den will be empty. In 2 Kings 2:24, a forensic team consisting of Samaritans and Hittites discover that the two bears can no longer be held responsible for devouring forty-two children. To top it off, the VeganBible will be printed on edible paper for those who decide to go back to the broad road that leads to destruction.

THE NARCISSIST BIBLE

This one will be available in stores in springtime 2036... or actually... it will be obtainable on demand. The personal pronoun "I" will be printed in the color red and will have exclamation marks in the same color. The "I am" texts from the Gospel of John will be followed by a dotted line so that the narcissist can write his own name there. This will relieve him from the injustice suffered by not seeing your own name in the Bible. The "each other" texts in the Pauline letters, speaking of joint harmony in marriage and in the church, have been stylishly blurred by our editors. If you preorder today, you'll get a bonus in the form of a personal songbook including classics such as "The Power of My Love," "Lord I Lift My Name on High," and "Great is My Faithfulness." For those who are more hands-on kind of folks, we have included a kit of the Tower of Babel so you can build a name for yourselves.

The Conspiracy Bible

As we speak, our designers are finishing up their book cover design. It has a photo of a serious looking Christ figure amid fire, brimstone, and some vague pictures of the galaxy. Unlike the other new Bibles, this one won't be available in brick-and-mortar stores. This will only be sold through obscure Telegram groups or through the dark web. We've carefully checked the audio version for any secret messages from the World Economic Forum, Bill Gates, Satan, or others who are ready to take over the world with force.

We've included a couple of extras for you to enjoy. You'll find a list of addresses of politicians who like to work from home and cannot wait until you are on their doorstep. We also added a grocery list if you want to prep for an alien invasion.

The Millenial Bible

This one is especially written for Millennials, those born in the eighties and nineties. In this cool edition, only the fun parts of the Bible remain. Most of the hard sayings from Jesus are rephrased so that it's possible to believe, fall away from the faith, and later come back to Jesus as your coach. He can be your savior, but there's an option to not acknowledge him as Lord.

You're invited to a middle of the road kind of faith á la carte where you can pick and choose what you want to believe and what you want to leave out. This edition will not stand in your way as you try to fulfil all your dreams within the next five years. Jesus won't ask anything of you so you can read it safely while having your first, second, or third burnout.

We've added some phrases to make sure Millennials feel at ease. You will read about Jesus chilling in the break room, and Elijah is characterized as totally basic. Moses has got a killer swag as he wanders through the desert, and you'll hear the disciples saying that the struggle is real when experiencing yet another beating.

Well, let's hope that God won't make all our dreams come true!

APRIL 10

A few of my flock visited Johan and Marjolein to convince them to go to Ahoy Rotterdam. A well-known American faith healer and his entire crew would be coming to Holland for a healing conference. Now that they've stopped the treatment, Salomé is gradually improving. She might be fit for the three-hour journey. Johan asked me for advice; should they stay at home or expect a miracle?

I came into conflict with myself. On the one hand, there's the vision I received at the park and our faithfulness to James 5, anointing her with oil and praying over her. On the other hand, I still hope that the vision was just a fruit of my imagination and that we all will live to see her grow up. But can miracles only happen through evangelists from overseas who own a private jet? Why not through some average joe Baptists around the corner?

I've said to Johan that it's up to him to make a choice, and I'm willing to drive them up to Rotterdam if they want to go.

They wrote me an email just now that they're going to take me up on the offer.

April 11

Don't know if I did the right thing yesterday. Shouldn't I have just said that charlatans like that faith healer prefer to take your money rather than giving you comfort? I once ended up at a healing crusade at the heart of the Dutch Bible Belt. After a short message, which was more like a pep talk, the healing train took off. The preacher received a heavenly vision that there were people present with unequal leg length and that the Lord was ready to release them from their suffering.

For an hour, people came on stage testifying they experienced something warm inside. It felt as if they were no longer in pain and the preacher thanked God for these great miracles of healing. There was even someone who was healed from sweaty hands. Down to earth person that I am, I wondered how you know you are healed from sweaty hands without doing some kind of workout.

The remarkable thing was that the conference center was right next to a hospice where I had to visit and accompany a forty-year-old father who would die quickly because the disease he carried almost cut his weight in half and slashed all his hopes and expectations for a long and happy life. Apparently, the Almighty does have time to heal sweaty hands and a bit of cartilage on the side, but a dying father leaves him cold.

I couldn't help but wonder if the organizing committee of this Healing and Restoration conference did not consider it strange to fill a stage with claimed healings of futilities while there were young people dying in the hospice next door.

Maybe I'm just afraid deep down that healing will come for Salomé, but not through my hands. That God will work through others, but not through me. We'll see. Maybe I can learn something from the preacher concerning stage presence in such a large auditorium.

APRIL 14

Deborah took me out for dinner today. We finally got a chance to reflect on our first months in Zwagerheide. Deborah puts down her cutlery and started talking with her mouth full. "Case, it seems like God is playing a simultaneous exhibition in your life right now, just like those great chess players do when they take on several opponents at the same time."

Somewhat surprised, I asked her to elaborate on that a bit more.

"Well, you initially thought this whole conference thing was a stepping stone for furthering your own little kingdom here in Holland. I could hear that in your voice from the moment you told me about the opportunity. There's no need to argue about this, Case. I know I'm right."

"I have to agree that you're on the right end of the stick. Now tell me a little bit more about that chessboard." I take a sip of my beer and brace myself.

"I think everything that has happened in our life in recent months serves a higher purpose. I think it will bring you to your knees and a step closer to where you need to be, Case. Maybe this isn't about you furthering your kingdom, but about Christ teaching you new things."

"Do you think I'll win the chess game, Deborah? Am I going to see the bigger plan, before I go up on that stage in May?" I said, slightly annoyed as I still felt she was talking in riddles.

"Honey, you know you can't beat Him. He plays chess on so many boards, and He thinks forty moves ahead. There's no chance you will overcome Him. A pawn has no chance against the King, sweetheart."

APRIL 19

I just got back from a trip to the city of Zwolle. Today, all the conference speakers of the Heaven and Earth conference gathered for a briefing. I had hoped that we could pitch our sermon outlines and talk about a theological framework. I was well prepared to pitch my idea around brokenness in the Christian life. It turned out differently, the story of my life really.

The briefing wasn't about content; it was a training in public speaking. A lovely young lady gave us the nuts and bolts about overcoming stage fright and how to impress a ten-thousand-person audience. I'll share some of her techniques with you.

* * *

First of all, we should aim to create some breathtaking moments during our sermon. According to her, it's crucial that our "talk" elicits a strong emotional response. It doesn't matter if it's fear, joy, shock, or surprise as long as there is an emotional response.

This took me back to the day when I was preaching at a youth event. I had prepared a talk on being born again, but the guy behind the laptop picked the wrong PowerPoint presentation. Instead of showing my slides on regeneration, sanctification, and glorification (folder Rebirth), the youngsters were provided with some rare footage of Deborah delivering our first child (folder Birth). I couldn't see the screen myself and the laptop guy was too busy with his phone. Although accidental, I must confess that it was breathtaking and life changing for most of the teenagers present.

The second technique we were encouraged to use was using humor without telling a joke. I consider myself well able to provide that. I started daydreaming while she was instructing the more boring speakers in the room to add a little more laughter to their sermons.

If this hadn't really happened, I wouldn't be able to make it up. When I was pastoring in Zwolle years ago, I had an associate pastor helping me out with the things I wasn't fond of doing. One day I decided to give him some leash. He could preach a sermon and choose the topic himself. He decided to preach on circumcision. He had learned in seminary that bringing in visual presentations could be helpful to prove your point. In secret, he had made a 2.5-meter-long penis from cardboard. He lived five kilometers from the church building and didn't have a car, so he took it under his arm and cycled all the way to church through the pouring rain. During his sermon, it became evident that the cardboard had suffered a bit from the torrential downpour. Just as he was coming down from the pulpit to explain the procedure of circumcision, the whole thing collapsed and hit the elders sitting in the front row. Most of our members comforted him and complimented him on the fact that he had the balls to try it.

Tip number 3. We should aim at including at least three stories or anecdotes in our sermon. Rumor has it that brain scans have shown that stories stimulate and involve the human brain like nothing else can. I think I have a few up my sleeve. If not, I can ask my uncle Vincent to come up with something. Note to self: I should make every effort to not let him know that I'm speaking at the conference!

Many more tips and techniques were exchanged today, some more helpful than others. After lunch I dosed off a bit and wondered how heaven relates to earth as it comes to speaking techniques and podium presence. Is heaven impressed if we use all these gimmicks? Is everyone on the edge of their heavenly seat when we preach a perfectly crafted sermon? A verse about the angels celebrating in heaven when one leaves the broad road of destruction came to mind. I don't know if there are any angels called Gerben or Tristan, but if there are, this is how their conversations might look on a Sunday morning.

* * *

"Hey Gerben, great to see you. What a privilege to work the Sunday morning shift with you. Sundays are easy, don't you think? I don't think anything strange will happen today. If only those preacher fellows would avail of those speaking techniques, we would be in for a treat, don't you think?"

"Don't know Tristan, I have high hopes for today, to be honest!"

They both sit down and look down to find a preacher somewhere who ticks all the boxes to provide a heavenly homecoming party.

After listening for a while, Tristan becomes a bit uneasy. "Gerben, wake up, were you counting like me? That preacher over there has already integrated two stories, he has made the people laugh without telling a joke, and one of those stories provoked an emotional response from the lady on the second row! Will this be the day that someone comes to faith?"

"Don't work yourself up, Tristan. It's like having one of those Christmas scratch-cards. You always get to twelve pine-branches, but you need thirteen to hit the jackpot. Let's wait and see what will happen, okay?"

Gerben continues to focus as tension rises. He is on the edge of his seat as he sees the orator taking the center of the stage, putting his feet slightly apart to simulate an open position. Tristan's expectations grow as well as the preacher supports his testimony with a YouTube clip including some melodramatic music. Both look over their shoulder to see if the Holy Spirit is already taking action to bring in inveterate unbelievers overcome by so much stage presence and speaking techniques.

"Tristan, I think we should take a step in faith: Let's cut the cake and poor the drinks, look at him!"

Both of the angels see the preacher stepping down from the pulpit, accentuating that he once was where the crowds are now. To top it off, the worship team sneaks onto the platform to play some background music for the final chapter: the altar call. Meanwhile, Tristan and Gerben have prepared for the obvious by putting on their party hats and blowing their party horns.

* * *

I hope you can forgive me for this sarcasm, but I'm still not convinced that speaking techniques will bring unbelievers into heaven. I think preaching the gospel, the waywardness of man, and the holiness of God is still the way to go about it instead of learning new tricks like some sort of puppy.

Deborah feels I'm overreacting. "Don't be so stubborn, Case. Take the best of both. You can preach the gospel and work on your podium presence simultaneously. There's nothing wrong with learning new things at your age, is there?"

I'll be meeting some colleagues at a pastor's fraternal tomorrow. Let's hear what they have to say about these things.

APRIL 20

Have you ever experienced that new information made you more confused than ever before? I was on my way to the pastor's fraternal when I spotted a hitchhiker on my left. I got the strong impression that this was the moment to do my random act of kindness for the day. When I got closer, I saw that it was Grandpa, and I slowed down. I quickly removed the paper cups, empty bags of M&M's, and other knickknacks from the passenger seat.

"Well, Case, thanks for being my good Samaritan. I was standing there for over half an hour, you know. This gives us some time to chat. I can imagine you have some unanswered questions regarding this old man. We bumped into each other a couple of times but haven't gotten a chance to really get to know one another."

I agreed that it was indeed time to satisfy my curiosity. "Sure, Grandpa. Let me ask you this. I saw you playing with little Salomé in church the other day and noticed you sitting in the conservatory while me and the elders were praying with her. How do you know them?"

"That's a long story, Case, and maybe a bit hard to understand, but I'll try to explain it to you the best I can. You see, it's my job to get alongside where I'm asked to come alongside. My boss thought it would be good to spend a little more time with Salomé and her parents in this particularly difficult season of their lives. That said, Case, I've always had a special connection with her."

I decided to ask the million-dollar questions. "Who is your boss? Are you employed by the hospital or a general practitioner?"

"No, Case, you are getting at the wrong end of the stick here. You might want to see me as some kind of ambassador. I was told that you spent several days in Ireland last year with Marcel and others. Picture it like this. In Dublin, you have the Dutch embassy. This embassy represents the Netherlands in Ireland. Her goal is to help the inhabitants of the kingdom of the Netherlands in a country that's foreign to them. In addition, they organize loads of activities to highlight the splendor of the Netherlands to the Irish to get them to long for spending some time over there.

"The position of the ambassador as such is therefore twofold. On the one hand, he helps the inhabitants of his own kingdom in the foreign country they're in; on the other hand he's a representative of the same kingdom in the middle of that foreign country. Well, that's pretty much my job and sums up what I do."

It felt like there were a bunch of crickets playing racquetball in between my ears. "Tell me then, Grandpa, you say you are an ambassador. But I've never seen one before playing in church with children they don't know. Which country do you represent and where are you residing? It can't be a wealthy country. The ambassadors I see on the news have a chauffeur and drive a Mercedes. I never saw one hitchhiking in rural Friesland before."

Grandpa laughed like a father who just shared a difficult riddle with his children that seems impossible to solve. "It's not that simple, Case. I represent a kingdom that is not officially recognized among people. You could say that this kingdom has no borders and that is difficult for many to understand. We don't drive luxury cars and are not in the business of climbing ladders of success like you people do. Although we have certain ranks and positions where I come from. Several of my coworkers have far more responsibilities than I do. But I must say that my role is growing as my king is making me into a specialist in a certain area.

"The most important thing for you to know is that I represent a kingdom which doesn't have an equal. Our king regularly sends us to places where there's a specific job for us to do. I'm assigned to this beautiful part of Friesland for the time being."

The crickets were still playing. The more he told me, the harder I found it to grapple with. "So, what is your assignment here in Friesland?"

"That too is not as simple as you might have hoped. Let me bring it a little closer. After you spent those wonderful days in Ireland, you decided that it was time to move on and moved from the county of Drenthe to Friesland. You then told a moving service to do the dirty work of packing boxes and moving furniture. We thought you made an excellence choice making that move, but that aside. You and your possessions were neatly brought from A to B. My client has used me to guide these kinds of processes. Within my team, I am the one who brings people from A to B.

"Moving is a stressful time for most people, Case. Especially the removals that I help to establish. You made a voluntary decision to move from Drenthe to Friesland, but I come across a lot of people who don't want to move and would rather stay put. Do you understand what I'm saying?"

The crickets were now playing doubles as I gazed out of the window.

"Can I ask you a question now, Case?"

"Sure, I promise I won't be beating around the bush like you, Grandpa."

"Great, you should know that your church isn't the only one I visit every now and then. I notice a change of thinking and wonder if you recognize it."

Somewhat annoyed, I asked for clarification.

"Well, let me put it this way. You all confess and sing that you can't wait to fly away to celestial shores where there are no tears and mourning to be found. That you will see Christ as He is, experience joy without limits, and will be walking the streets of gold. But in your prayers, I hear a completely different message. You pray for healing, recovery, extended life here on earth, and things like that. This seems a bit paradoxical to me. You seem to be praying for longevity on earth instead of the joy of reaching heaven. That's a bit strange, isn't it? I've seen exceptions, of course, but it seems you prefer earth over heaven."

I must confess that it's easier to sing about celestial shores when they're nowhere to be seen than when we are getting awfully close. We often encourage each other with the promise that the best is yet to come, but when the best seems to have come, we try to back out of it with everything that is in us.

"You know, Grandpa, although we are believers, we are still human, just like you, so don't expect too much from us, okay?"

"I know you are, Case, trust me. Could you drop me off here? I'm where I need to be."

I turned on the warning lights and parked on the side of the road so Grandpa could step out of the car. "Is this the place where you are working on another assignment that I don't understand?"

"You could put it that way indeed. I see you are puzzled, but rest assured, this will all make more sense to you in a couple of weeks' time, I promise you. Your questions will be answered then, but new ones will emerge. That's part of life for earthly beings. I can't take that away from you. Before I forget, I'll be there in Ahoy Rotterdam but will take care of my own transport. I'll see you then."

APRIL 25

This morning in church we announced our trip to Ahoy Rotterdam later this week. After the service, I received a mixed response. Most of the people present didn't think it was a good idea to give the Boersma family false hope.

Salomé is alternating between bad days and very bad days. She was too tired to play in the back of the church and sat on Grandpa's lap for most of the service. Maybe it was my imagination, but it looked like he had tears in his eyes. His look was very determined. What a character. Still not sure what to think of him.

April 28

Words can't describe how I feel right now. This day supplied me with enough material to write another book, but I'll stick to a quick summary for now.

Tensions rose as we drove to Rotterdam today. Marjolein mentioned that she has the same feeling as when going to Groningen Hospital for another scan or treatment, living life between hope and fear. Salomé was in great spirits today, singing kids' praise songs nonstop until we got there.

An hour before the doors opened, we arrived at Ahoy. The rate at which time passes depends on your reference. Watching a football game for an hour is much easier than being in a crowd with a group of people with a mixture of expectation, despair, and hope running through their veins.

Once inside, we were all led into a kind of funnel so that we could not avoid the registration tables. Johan and Marjolein had a lot of questions to answer about Salomé's official diagnosis, treatment, and life expectancy. After they filled in all the forms, we were taken to our allocated seats by a friendly man. We were left of the main stage, tucked away in the back of the room. It struck me as odd that our section was filled with people who were very sick. I saw many young and old on whom chemo had left its mark. They were joined by people missing limbs; others were in electric wheelchairs.

In the section right in front of the main stage, there were people who seemed less ill. They talked to each other, joked, and were able to get out of their seats to let others pass. I wonder if the same would have happened in Jesus's days. Who would He be closest to?

In the meantime, I browsed through the magazine we received upon entering. Most of the articles were written by today's miracle worker. He wanted us to claim our miracle and walk in our destiny. The response card inside encouraged us to sow our money so we'll reap a harvest. I saw the countdown starting on a big screen. The event would start in five minutes, tension was rising. The stage fog machines were working overtime, as were the musicians who came from overseas to get the worship going. They certainly seemed to know what they were doing; the music was great. Accompanied by a full gospel choir acting as background vocals, they helped us to expect the impossible tonight and not to think too small of God. The four of us sang, and Salomé even did a little dance. Our expectations were growing.

After singing their last song, they walked offstage. This was where the prophet, healer, and revivalist Jeffrey John and his translator entered the stage.

I had asked Marcel to tell me more about him earlier this week. He indicated that he had worked with Jeffrey at various healing conferences in Europe in recent years and that he's a very likeable brother. "Case, I must say that in the past year, I've changed my mind on many things. I look differently at the whole ministry of healing and restoration as well. Still, I think it's a good thing for you to experience it yourself, without my opinion in mind. Just go with the flow with this one, okay?"

John took the center of the stage, where he clearly felt at home. He was neatly dressed, well cut and cared for. His tanned skin suggested a tanner had been smuggled into his luggage. He shared some testimonies about miraculous healings that happened in Budapest just a few days ago and urged us to believe that Christ can do the impossible for us tonight: "Don't limit Him! He can only work the miracles you expect Him to do. If you don't believe you will be healed, I'm afraid there's nothing He can do for you tonight."

That seemed to put a lot of pressure on people who were crushed already, but I considered that maybe it was that my faith was too small.

After thirty minutes of preaching, Jeffrey asked the

musicians back on stage. The synthesizer strings provided a constant background sound, and the strumming guitar topped it off. The atmosphere was charged. Now was the time! The sick were invited to come forward, where Jeffrey and his team would pray for them. "God has something much better for you than a sick body. Come and receive your healing!" he shouted from the top of his lungs.

Marjolein looked at Johan with hope in her eyes as he carried little Salomé toward the stage. For each section, there was a gatekeeper responsible for some sort of final screening. When Johan moved to the front end of our part, he was stopped. He was informed that the committee had decided that those in our section were not allowed to go up for prayer. I could see Johan arguing with the security guard, who was much smaller than him. I could see his anger increasing. He was almost face-to-face with the man while holding Salomé close to his chest. It was like one of those stare downs on television. The spiritual fruit of self-control is more abundant with Johan than with me. I don't know if I would be able to refrain from violence like Johan did.

I see the despair in Marjolein's eyes as he walked back to his seat. "Johan, why are you back here and not with Jeffrey over there?"

"We are not allowed to go upfront, honey. They've determined that people from this section can't go on camera. Jeffrey would like to meet us afterward at the book table to shake our hands, but we shouldn't expect much more than that tonight."

While Marjolein put her head against Johan's chest, crying with bewilderment and anger, Johan put Salomé in her own chair. But she was not alone. Grandpa embraced her. "It will soon be over, sweetheart. He wants you to be where He is. Trust me, it's beautiful there. The next time you see me, you can come with me, okay? Your new home is almost finished."

As I heard Grandpa speaking those words of comfort, I noticed Salomé couldn't take her eyes off him as he put a smile on her tired face. He gave her a kiss on the forehead and then left. I saw him going back and forth through our section, comforting people who were astonished, just like we are.

When Marjolein's tears had run dry, she asked me to get the car. She'd seen enough. We all had. All of us were quiet as the lights of our car penetrated the dark skies. None of us said a word, except for Salomé. "I want to go home, Daddy."

"We're almost there, love, just a few more minutes and Pastor Case will drop us off, okay?"

I couldn't help to think that she was talking about a different home. I was beginning to sense that Grandpa would be influential in getting there.

APRIL 29

The day after. On my Facebook feed, I came across the after movie of the healing service. Four minutes of spiritual fireworks where I see crutches going up, reading glasses trampled on, and unequal legs being restored to the former glory of equality after one touch from Jeffrey John.

I didn't see any people from our section. The more I watched, the angrier I got. I was seriously thinking of giving Jeffrey a piece of my mind. This shouldn't be swept under the carpet.

"Don't throw the child away with the bathwater and don't hit back." Deborah was right.

I believe God can heal in our days. It could also be true that Jeffrey is a nice guy, and that God uses him for His purposes.

Johan sent me a text to say that they really appreciated that I drove them all the way to Rotterdam yesterday. They were sorry it turned out this way. I'm sorry too.

MAY 3

I still haven't settled on what to speak on at the conference. By now I would've expected some clear revelation from the heavenlies. I can't make a fool out of myself by stuttering and stumbling the whole way through.

Marcel put me at ease this afternoon. We spent some time reflecting on what happened in Rotterdam, but most of all, we talked about the upcoming highlight of my ministry.

"Case, let it go, will you? You're your own worst enemy. It's like saying to yourself, at 2 a.m., that you must sleep, otherwise tomorrow will be a bad day. The more you say it, the harder it gets to wind down and doze off. Have you ever been lost for words in the pulpit? He knows what you need, and He will provide".

I am still determined to talk about God's nearness in suffering. I'll probably get it all together just before I walk onto the stage. If he can speak through donkeys in the Old Testament, He will be able to do it through me, I suppose.

MAY 4

It's late, I can't sleep. Today will go down in history as the day heaven touched earth. At least for those present. Only a few have seen what I witnessed today. And all who did will utterly fail to describe what they've seen, heard, and felt when it happened. As I'm writing this, I feel like Luke, the writer of the Book of Acts, trying to describe what happened in the upper room during Pentecost. There are not sufficient or satisfactory words, but I'll give it a try. I hope it will be enough to make you long for Home.

I got a call, early in the morning from Johan. He asked if I could come as soon as possible. "It looks like Salomé will not make it through the day, Pastor. The doctor has already been here, and the nurse will stay for as long as she needs. She was very restless last night and has been given extra pain medication that has put her to sleep. They don't expect her to wake up again. Marjolein and I are watching over her, and we would appreciate if you'd be here as well."

I promised Johan to come over straightaway and woke up Deborah to give her an update. After we prayed, she quickly prepared me a sandwich that I ate on my way up. I have often been near a deathbed, but never before with someone as young as Salomé. As I cycled, my head was working overtime. I dedicated some of my darker thoughts to Jeffrey John and prayed for healing at the same time as I biked the cobblestone roads of Zwagerheide. I thought about the vision I saw in the park the other day. Salomé Boersma in a beautiful white dress. Her hair wavy to her shoulders, her charming smile. She laughed like a child does when her father tickles her until she can't take it any longer. Her arms without an IV, her neck without a Rainbow Trail.

As I rang the bell, I saw a dim light burning in the conservatory. The town was still asleep, but those present were wide awake.

Strangely enough, I entered a peace contrary to the circumstances. Johan had moved her adapted bed to the conservatory, next to the pellet stove. Salomé was asleep. The soft tones of some of the quieter kids' praise songs were playing in the background. She was surrounded by all her favorite cuddly toys. The warmth of the stove helped to overcome the spells of cold fever she suffered last night. She looked comfortable.

The three of us gave each other a hug before I took a seat. Together, we sat for over half an hour without saying a word. We were keeping our thoughts to ourselves and were praying in silence.

Marjolein broke the silence. "You know, Brother Parker, I

know people are praying for us. We've stopped praying for healing but are now asking Him to spare her from unnecessary suffering. That's okay, right?"

I assured Marjolein that it was an act of confidence in the providence of God and certainly not a sign of unbelief. We thanked God for being near to us after reading Psalm 23, a psalm dear to the family. Johan took Salome's hand. "He knows love, He knows."

The peace that transcends all understanding slowly took hold of us. If God indeed collects our tears in his bottle, there must have been angels running around like crazy to gather some more bottles, or probably buckets. The peace felt and the tears cried go hand in hand. The nurse checked her saturation and noticed that the little one's breathing had become irregular. "It won't be long, Marjolein," she said.

Time is relative. Those seconds must have felt like an hour and those minutes like years from their perspective. The nurse left us to it and sat at the kitchen table making her notes.

Then it happened. If I hadn't been there myself, I would've found it hard to believe.

Suddenly, there was a sound that increased in strength. It sounded like a takeoff from one of the F-35 fighter jets at the military air base in Leeuwarden. Every Tuesday, they fly over Zwagerheide, doing their training rounds. What started off with a soft hum became louder and louder as Salome's struggle with breathing increased. It was almost deafening, but there was more. The well-insulated house of the Boersma's could not prevent a gentle breeze coming through, which went up to gale force within twenty seconds. Even the flame in the stove was struggling. It seemed that the sound and the wind were working toward a grand finale.

We looked at each other in amazement but didn't panic. What followed probably would have taken only a few seconds, but it was as if it were in slow motion.

Suddenly, Salomé sat up in her bed. At first sight, I wondered if it was really her. The brown circles and bags under her eyes had gone. Her hair was back and even longer than when I first met her. I saw what I had seen in my vision, and now Johan and Marjolein were allowed to see it too. Her beautiful blue eyes carried a mixture of anticipation and joy as she looked at Johan and Marjolein. "Mommy, Daddy... I can go home now, He's here!"

All both could say, with tears in their eyes, was, "Go on, honey. It's all right."

Unexpectedly, Johan and I saw a familiar face. It was the man who was waiting for him at his van the other day. It was the ambassador, sent from above to move people to a better place. It was Salome's playmate. The man who often left me with more questions than answers. It was Grandpa. He looked relieved, determined, and ready for what needed to happen.

Delighted, he walked to the bed and took her in his arms. His eyes met hers and together they danced and spun around through the conservatory. Salomé threw her head back, and Grandpa cried tears of joy.

Today was the day they could both go home. Salomé can take up residence there; Grandpa can catch his breath before his next assignment. Together they walked toward the conservatory door, open it, and fly toward the rising sun. The last thing we heard was her laugh.

The wind decreased, the sound turned into a whisper before it faded out. The nurse came in, completely ignorant of what had just happened. For two minutes she checked for a pulse and then determined what we already knew. Salomé is at Home where she belongs.

MAY 9

The days flew by. I was reminded of that iconic picture, taken just after the terror attack on Bruxelles airport a few years ago. A flight attended with torn clothes, surrounded by debris, gazes into a camera with her mouth open in astonishment. That's how I feel right now.

Today was the thanksgiving service for Salome's life. Around half past ten, Deborah and I headed over to the Boersmas. Marjolein was dressed in a beautiful, colored dress, and Johan also looked his best. We put our coats down on the stairway in the hall, and we could smell the freshly baked apple pie.

"Thanks for spending this morning with us. Salomé is in the conservatory. Maybe you want to go in?"

We walk over, but I'm hesitant. I would rather have remembered her in her full strength, flying toward her new home with Grandpa and hearing her laughter. Deborah and Marjolein give each other a long hug. Johan and I pat each other on the back like only men can do who want to show affection but don't know how to go about it.

There she was. Laying in a Moses basket, surrounded by all her cuddly toys. A basket like Jochebed put Moses in before saying her goodbyes, not knowing that she would get him back eventually. Salomé looked beautiful. She was wrapped in linen, just like Christ, the greater Moses, was after He carried all our sickness, sin, and shame. This basket and linen blanket won't be the end of her journey.

We go to the kitchen and eat apple pie. "Remember, Pastor, when you first came here? When I asked you how you drink your coffee, you joked that you only drink your coffee with apple pie. This is a great day to provide you with everything you need. We are very grateful for how you've helped us along these last months.

I pulled out all the stops to eat anything today. I already skipped breakfast and made every effort to eat and enjoy that apple pie.

"We are so glad you didn't bombard us with similar experiences from churches you served before or other stuff. Nothing stays with us anyway. You just sat with us, listened, and returned what you've heard us say in prayer toward God. That was all we needed."

Time passed by slowly. No hearses or printed liturgies with a black lining today.

"Marjolein and I would like to have some time together to close the basket if that's okay with you".

"Of course, Johan. Case and I will wait for you in the hallway. Go ahead."

Fifteen minutes later, they came out of the conservatory. Johan with the basket in his strong arms and Marjolein with a few cuddly toys in her hands. The four of us took our seats in Johan's new Mercedes van. Johan and I in the front, our wives in the back with the Moses basket safely between them. The drive was only a short one. We drove slowly through the town and were greeted by many villagers with a look of understanding and sadness in their eyes. Most of them would soon be getting ready for the condolence. Tragedies like this bring towns together, it's bittersweet, but it's true.

Johan carried the basket into the church. I think of a photo I saw on their wall, taken somewhere in a zoo. The little one enjoying her ice cream, sitting on her dad's shoulders. Could Johan have thought that one day he wouldn't carry her on his shoulders, but in a basket?

Just about the whole town showed up to give Johan and Marjolein their support. The other toddlers from kindergarten brought some drawings. Marjolein collected them all and looked at them like they'd all produced a Van Gogh. She put them on the basket, along with the many flowers.

Later than planned, we started the thanksgiving service. I heard myself talking about the God who is close to the brokenhearted, tears collected in His bottle and realized that this was a tryout for next week's conference.

Johan and Marjolein shared some wonderful memories and showed some family photos, which made us laugh and cry at the same time. But neither said a word about those last few minutes in the conservatory when heaven touched earth in a spectacular way. Just as wine and whiskey get better as they mature, so do experiences like this. Some things we should keep to heart, just like Mary did, for the time being.

As we sang Salome's favorite song, Johan and Marjolein walked toward the Moses basket, grabbed its handles, and walked toward the door with a sorrowful look on their faces.

"Thanks, Pastor, you did well."

I took in the compliments of some of our members. They were right, not so much about me, but it was as good as it gets if it comes to funerals. The Lord was in it.

The burial itself was private. Only Johan, Marjolein, some close relatives and Deborah and I travel to the cemetery I visited upon arriving in Zwagerheide a few months ago. As we arrived, we walked toward the grave, which was really only a hole someone dug. We know this is only temporary until she will rise again clothed with the imperishable. We prayed the Lord's prayer, and we lowered Salomé into the grave. As we did, we heard the laughter of children playing hide-and-seek on the corner of Church Lane and Baker Street.

"Case and I will head on; we'll leave you to it okay? Don't hesitate to call us or come over. You are welcome twenty-four/seven."

I shook Johan's hand, and we walked back to the church. The gravel creaked under our feet. When I looked over my shoulder, I saw Johan grab a shovel to fill up the grave again.

MAY 11

Another forty-eight hours before I set foot on the main stage. I must confess that I didn't feel up for the challenge of confronting thousands of ecstatic believers with my out-of-the-box preaching. I asked Deborah if it wouldn't be better to call in sick. She gave me a fiery look and told me it was a little late for running scared. I called Johan yesterday, and he encouraged me to go and be myself.

Marcel stopped by tonight and urged me to take a rest, spend time with God and not with my commentaries. "It's better to receive it straight from the Father than from what others have said, Parker."

MAY 13

I was wide awake, way too early. It was 3:30 a.m. Deborah was still asleep. The birds had started their early morning routine of praising the One who cares for them. I am of more value than they are. I read that yesterday while walking through the park. That old familiar feeling of nerves, abdominal pain, and bowel movements took hold of me again. I wonder why on earth I said yes to this invitation. Why did I make my own life so miserable?

I got out of bed and pondered which clothes to put on. I really felt the need to be myself today on stage. Deborah convinced me yesterday that no one has ever appeared on such a stage wearing sweatpants and Nike Air Max and that she will do everything to prevent me from being the first. There goes authenticity! In marriage, you must choose your battles if you want to finish better than you've started.

So, I decided to put on what she had prepared for me. Blue trousers, white shirt, and a neat jacket to camouflage the few extra pounds I've gained these last couple of months. I recently saw a photo of Charles Spurgeon; he was struggling with his weight too but was still nicknamed the Prince of Preachers. If it worked for him, it would work for me.

There's one prayer that has helped me through a lot of difficulties in life. I let it roll over my lips daily. "May the words of my mouth and the meditation of my heart be acceptable in your sight, O Lord, my Rock and my Redeemer" (Psalm 19:15). A prayer through which I remind myself that He is big, and I am small. That I live my life for him, that He calls the shots. That I'm the receiver, but He remains the Provider.

I walked down the stairs. No coffee for me today. Caffeine and my bowels are not a good match, especially not in times of stress. In the kitchen, I made myself a sandwich, which I'll eat when I arrive. My body was in fight-or-flight mode, which in my case meant that it wanted to travel as light as possible.

I did some last-minute preparation, erased some words, and added some new ones. Ludovico Einaudi's modern classic music was on autoplay. Marcel recently told me a story about Isaac Stern, another gifted musician.

After one of his violin concerts in New York, a middle-aged lady approached him. "Mr. Stern, I would give my life if I could play like you."

"Well, I gave my life to play like me," he answered.

Excelling in something means you must sacrifice other things. I wouldn't call myself an excellent preacher, by the way. Who am I to be preaching for thousands today? God probably knows what He's doing. At least He permits it to happen. Let that be enough for now. I'll do my best and God will do the rest.

As I printed my sermon, I could hear Marcel's Volvo V70 pulling up in the driveway. Marcel jokes that we will eventually all end up with a car with a driver. Today, he wanted to grant me the pleasure of experiencing it while my feet were still warm. It was 5 a.m. as we left Zwagerheide behind us and drove up to the conference site, where the first prayer warriors were probably already engaged in intercession for lost people groups and the service for this morning. Deborah and the kids would be coming later.

We didn't say much along the way. Marcel, ex-celebrity pastor, knew exactly what was going on inside of me. He was where I am now. He let me gaze quietly across the fields and enjoy the rising sun. I recalled an important lesson Cornelius O'Hallihan, our retreat leader in Ireland, taught us. "Case, most pastors are made for the shadows and not for the broad daylight. Be careful when people tell you it's your time to shine."

I remember Eileen's words, spoken at Tramore's cemetery. "Look around you, Case. In these graves there are people who thought they were indispensable and who took themselves way too seriously. We are only little weak men and women in the hands of a powerful and almighty God." Her Irish wisdom that you don't have the fear the ill wind if your haystacks are tied down, touched my heart again. Knowing who you are in Christ is the true and only foundation.

While Marcel smoothly directed his Swedish powerhouse across the provincial boundaries, I opened my Bible and began to read Ephesians. I let the truth sink in that I was already loved and chosen before the foundations of the earth were laid. I'm chosen to be His beloved. I've received forgiveness for my sins, and part of my inheritance is already deposited in my account. In the distance, I saw rows of pop-ups, caravans, and festival tents of different proportions. We made it.

We introduced ourselves, shook some hands, and were taken to a cozily furnished unit for the final briefing. The floor manager, identifiable because of his headset, sweaty forehead, a box of sweets at hand, and an extra set of batteries in case the countdown clock isn't working, took the lead.

"Brother Parker, you have thirty minutes for your talk, okay? Please don't stretch it, I'm not the guy you want to offend," he said with a smile on his face but a strange twitch in his eye. He went on about the offering, the time for prayer, and a whole load of other things. The worship leader, wearing sweatpants and trainers, joked that the Holy Spirit loves to work in confined spaces like the floor manager had just provided. I liked the guy; I'm sure Deborah and his wife would love to have a chat about authenticity.

I think about Salomé. Her Rainbow Trail with too many beads, her head with not enough hair. I try to recall that early morning showdown between heaven and earth and succeed. It puts my mind to rest.

When it's almost time, I look and see crowds of people leaving the campsite and moving toward the tent of meeting. They're telling stories, laughing, kicking a ball, and enjoying the company of like-minded people. There's a traffic jam on the road to the conference. People from all tribes, tongues, and nations were coming over. Believers from rural areas like Zwagerheide would worship with those from African churches from the city-center of Amsterdam. As it will be in heaven.

During our pre-service prayer time, we prayed that heaven would touch earth this morning. Some prayed for a strong anointing on Br. Parker and a hedge of protection around him. I hoped the enemy wouldn't bring his garden tools to cut through that hedge. But this was not the time to tell one of my jokes.

Marcel approached the throne of grace with a final prayer, "Lord, may the words of Case's mouth and the meditations of his heart be acceptable in your sight, Amen!"

Heaven touches earth. We got up off our knees and the floor manager opened the door. He put an awfully tight headset around my head. I felt every touch, every word was coming in hard. But this form of stress was the healthy kind. There was enough adrenaline to help me perform but not enough to paralyze me.

We walked into the tent of meeting toward the first row. There was no turning back now. It wouldn't be long before I walked those stairs toward the stage. I stopped near row 10 as I spotted Deborah, the kids, and an unexpected visitor: Uncle Vincent. "Son, if you blackout, I have a few tricks up my sleeve to make this one to be remembered, so don't worry, okay?"

I assured him that this time I would do everything I could to brutally knock him out before he could even think of one of his dark jokes. We both laughed. I hoped this service would do what I couldn't: bring him to his knees.

We stepped over a bunch of cables attached to the floor with tape and sat—me, Marcel, and the floor manager. I scanned the stage for a lectern, and it was there, thankfully. Always handy to hold on to when you feel dizzy or to hide behind when you don't know exactly what to do with your body while preaching.

The drummer got the band rolling as we sang "Shine, Jesus, Shine." As I looked back, I met the eyes of Deborah, reassuring me that all would be well. The tent was packed; there were even people watching outside on a big screen. I mumbled along with the lyrics and clapped my hands at the appointed times. I had both my feet on earth, but my head was in heaven. "Give rest, Lord. In my breathing, in my bowels, in my thoughts."

During our training in Zwolle, I received the bonus tip to visualize my audience naked when the anxiety would become too much to bear. That is supposed to relieve stress. I tried that recently while preaching in my own church, but I found that it frightened me even more. I decided to preach without any form of visualization today.

The last song before the sermon was near the end and would fade out soon. Marcel put his hand on my back and said one last prayer in a language I'd never heard. The sweaty floor manager urged me to take a seat next to the stairs.

The worship leader started his introduction, "Dear brothers

and sisters, it's my privilege to introduce brother Case Parker to you. He was born and raised in County Drenthe, but now lives and works in Friesland so that His name will be great among the nations. He spent some time in Ireland and lived to tell the story. His first book caused a bit of controversy among the sheep but also managed to touch hearts. Today he will open the Scriptures on the theme: When Heaven Touches Earth. Please welcome him with a round of applause and show your appreciation for Case Parker!!!"

This was it. I walked onto the stage and managed to do so without tripping and falling over backward. I was still a bit nervous as I tapped my microphone to see if it was on. The bright spotlights made my eyes contract and made the crowds disappear. It was only me and the people in the first two rows it seemed.

"Stop clapping, beloved. You'll be in for a whole lot of trouble when I start to believe all the nice things he said about me."

That joke broke the ice, and I felt much more relaxed than before. I opened my Bible and put my sermon on the lectern. The tension seemed to be gone, no strange bowel movements. Another thirty minutes and it would all be over. I noticed on my smartwatch that my heart rate was up but not erratic.

"Beloved, this morning I want to take a few moments to ponder on some Scriptures where heaven touches earth. I don't want to ruin the party, but I've noticed that heaven especially touches earth when there appears to be suffering and brokenness. The Lord is specifically near the brokenhearted and the contrite in spirit. It is those who are poor in spirit who will see God. It's the mourning who will be comforted, and the hungry who will be satisfied."

I talk about Job, about Moses sitting by the well, and a weeping Jeremiah. About Joseph's journey from pit to palace. About Stephen, who sees heaven opening while heavy rocks crush his body. I elaborate on Peter, who is said to have been crucified upside down because he did not consider himself worthy of dying the same death as his Lord. I talk about the suffering servant who sweats tears of blood and seeks and finds God's nearness in His own deep darkness. I read from the Gospel of John and hear Jesus say that if they persecuted Him, that they'll come after us as well. I tell people that all our tears will be wiped away by the only hands in heaven that have scars on them.

With everything I had, I tried to convince people that suffering is a vital part of life for those who follow Christ. Because He himself had suffered and promised us that on this side of eternity we'll have to go through it as well to reap the benefits from it.

Halfway through my message, I saw someone standing next to Marcel. He was talking to the floor manager and seemed to have a handwritten note in his hands. The floor manager nervously looked to Marcel, who seemed to be persuading him to loosen up a bit and let God take control.

The man in the middle now moved toward the stage. Marcel and the floor manager were giving me a thumbs up. As he approached me, the confusion in the first row made sense now. It was the man with magic hands, the carpenter, whose action spoke louder than words. The man with sorrows who had a tale to tell. He looked tired but controlled. He was still mourning but on a mission. I told him to come up, and the floor manager gave him a handheld microphone. Johan Boersma was about to make his debut as a public speaker, and he would pass with flying colors.

He put his paper on the lectern and started to read out loud, ignoring all the things you learn at speaker training. I got the feeling that the angels were on the edge of their seat, even though he wouldn't take the center of the stage with a carefully crafted tearjerker.

Everyone was quiet and curious about the stranger. I heard people sobbing as he talked about what happened the morning Salomé passed away. How God's spirit was moving and how His presence was tangible. How Grandpa showed up and told her that her home in heaven was ready for her. The deafening noise, the beautiful white dress, the blissful look of a child who finished her ordeal of suffering at the appointed time. About gold found in the muck and mire and God's nearness to the brokenhearted.

"Dear brothers and sisters. There are people in our town saying that there cannot be a God because of what we had to go through. How would a loving God allow these things to happen? But I want to echo the words of my pastor: Where did He promise that He'd straighten every curve and fix every problem? Where did He say He would put us on a cruise ship so that the battering waves can't hurt us? Did He ever say that we would always be prosperous and would never suffer like others do? He didn't say that, did He? What He did say was that He would never leave, nor forsake us and that temporary setbacks produce character, fruit, and every other good thing under heaven in our lives.

"This is our testimony: He has been there every step of the way. He has shown us in more ways than you can ever imagine that He is faithful. He has fulfilled every promise. He was there that morning, and He is still here in our valley of tears. I hope you don't ever have to experience what we did, but if it happens, I hope you're carried in the same everlasting arms that we were carried with. Salomé is at home, and one day we'll be there also."

Johan picked up his notes and walked off stage. You could hear a pin drop. The earth wasn't shaking, no fire from the sky or the deafening noise of the wind. God revealed himself in the gentle whisper of His people.

The lights had dimmed, and I could see the crowd again. I

could feel the emotions of thousands, the recognition of hundreds, and the despair of a few. I saw Deborah, the kids. Even Uncle Vincent was listening breathlessly.

Someone walked in from the rear of the tent. He immediately caught my attention. He was in his late fifties, had gray hair and blue eyes. Some have entertained angels without knowing it is what Scripture teaches. But I know better now. I know Grandpa didn't come here for me. He had heard better sermons, I'm sure.

Halfway through, he took a left turn. He passed my children and Deborah and took the only empty seat in the entire tent. It was the chair next to Uncle Vincent. I saw them talking to each other. From there, it looked like they had known each other for years, and perhaps that was the case looking at it from Grandpa's perspective. The look in his eyes was the same as when I first saw him playing with Salomé in the back of the church. A look of joy, determination, his eyes fixed on the prize and the assignment given.

I ended with prayer and knew that I had nailed my colors to the mast. As the musicians came back on stage, Grandpa and I exchanged one more look. His expression told me everything I needed to know. Grandpa might still be a stranger to Uncle Vincent, but that wouldn't be for long. Their meetings would intensify. I prayed that their chats would convince Vincent of all the things we have said to him down through the years.

Gizmo and Gremlin will probably need to find a different place to live as Vincent will be changing residence. There will be no more teardrops falling on photographs from the past. There, he will see that Jesus has saved the best wine for last. What a day that will be! Heaven will soon be enriched by a stand-up comedian when the Good Shepherd will take this black sheep under his arm and puts him in between the other ninety-nine. On that day, heaven will touch earth again, I'm sure.

When the service was finished, the tent emptied. On the

festival grounds, I saw people praying, others walking alone and taking some time to reflect. Some came up and complimented me on my teaching this morning. Johan went home straight after his testimony. Wise man.

Uncle Vincent introduced me to his new friend.

"I enjoyed your sermon, Case; you should speak from the heart more often."

I smile and promise Grandpa I will.

Marcel dropped me off at home around nine o'clock. Deborah and the kids had arrived a few hours earlier. She said I made her proud today. I thanked her for telling me what I needed to hear during preparation. She and Marcel were the true prophets, I was their spokesperson.

"Can I wear my sweatpants now, love?"

Deborah told me I could, and we crashed on the couch. She surprised me with my favorite late-night dish: a bag of M&M's and a Guinness. We watched a British detective that we've probably seen before, but at our age, you can taste the joy of seeing an episode twice without remembering who did it. We didn't make it to the end. Deborah fell asleep after about thirty minutes. I switched to the football channel. Happy days.

Dear wondrous Diary,

Now that I've entrusted all this to your pages, I realize one thing: I don't care anymore if you will become the archaeological find of the century or if you end up in the bargain section of a Christian bookshop. I may have started off somewhat proud and arrogant, but I think I've learned my lesson. God knows my weaknesses. Your reader will know them too, wondrous diary.

I visited Salomé's grave today. There was only one word carved in the beautiful handcrafted wooden cross at her temporary place of rest: "Home." That's what I want on my tombstone. That settles it for me.

Deborah and I had coffee with Johan and Marjolein yesterday. Her belly is blooming beautifully. Six more weeks until her due date. They're expecting a boy. I suggested that Case would be a great name. Deborah pinched my inner thigh when I proposed that brilliant idea, don't know why.

I finally answered all the emails I got from conference guests. Their stories touched my heart. Many expressed that they experience room for brokenness as they have shed their tight armor of ever-conquering faith. Deborah and Marcel were right. I made a public confession on a podcast last week that I didn't like the idea initially, but that they kept pushing through. Honor where credit is due.

Uncle Vincent called this week. He has had some bad news from the doctor. He will come over for lunch tomorrow. Stew with brown beer. Deborah said he could bring Gizmo and Gremlin and his belongings to stay over for as long as he wants. He took her up on the offer and will move in with us. It could get quite uncomfortable, wondrous diary, when he decides to join in on the many pastoral conversations we have at home. Ah well, we'll see. Hope to see you tomorrow.

THE END

About the Author

Kees Postma is a Dutch pastor and church planter living in the rural north of Holland. He likes playing his $50 guitar, watching good comedies, playing darts and going for long walks. His favorite holiday destination is Ireland where he lived for over four years. Find out more and subscribe to his newsletter at **www.keespostma.com**

Please review this book

If this book has helped you in any way, please leave an online review at the retailer you bought it, on Goodreads or another platform. As a beginning author word of mouth really helps, especially in the niche that I'm writing for. Thanks again!

Grab another one in this series: The Retreat: A light-hearted and humorous story about a soul-searching Pastor (Part I)

The RETREAT

KEES POSTMA

A light hearted and humorous story
ABOUT A SOUL SEARCHING PASTOR

Case Parker, a worn-out pastor, is shocked by all the good, bad, and ugly he has found in pastoral ministry so far. He constantly asks himself this question: Should I stay, or should I go? Having reached a point of utter exhaustion he decides to go to Ireland for a three-day retreat. Case, and the other Dutch shepherds that join him, end up in all kinds of interesting, dangerous, and hilarious situations. This story will have you in stitches, will make you feel convicted and hopefully has you changed by the time the story ends.

Made in the USA
Las Vegas, NV
31 July 2023

75498549R00065